Schools in the Learning Age

Edited by Bill Lucas and Toby Greany

CAMPAIGN
FOR **LEARNING**

Our thanks go to all the contributors, especially Michael Barber and Bob Fryer, who initiated the debate on schools and lifelong learning at the Campaign's annual RSA Lecture in March 2000. Thanks also go to all the teachers involved in the Campaign's Learning to Learn action research project, which is beginning to show how some of the ideas contained here could work in practice. Finally, thanks to the Canadian Education Association and Education Canada, in which a version of John Abbott and Terry Ryan's article first appeared.

Copyright © Text Campaign for Learning

First published in 2000 by the
Campaign for Learning
19, Buckingham Street
London WC2N 6EF

Produced for the Campaign for Learning by
Southgate Publishers
The Square
Sandford
Nr Crediton
Devon EX17 4LW

All rights reserved. No part of this publication may be reproduced, copied or transmitted in any form or by any means, electronic, mechanical, photocopying, recording or otherwise, without the prior written permission of the publisher or in accordance with the Copyright, Design and Patents Act 1988.

Printed and bound in Great Britain by Short Run Press, Exeter, Devon

British Library Cataloguing in Publication Data
A CIP catalogue record for this book is available from the British Library

ISBN 1 903107 10 5

Contents

Schools and lifelong learning tomorrow

Foreword

Rt Hon David Blunkett MP, Secretary of State for Education and Employment

MY TOP PRIORITIES ON BECOMING Secretary of State for Education and Employment were to publish our strategies for raising school standards and for creating a lifelong learning society in the UK. In the Foreword to *The Learning Age* I referred to learning's power not only to secure our economic future, but to help us fulfil our potential, promote active citizenship and make ours a more civilised society.

I stand by that belief in the power of learning and I am pleased that so many people have worked so hard over the past three years to begin to make it a reality for all. Standards are rising in schools, while initiatives such as *learndirect* (Ufl Ltd), Individual Learning Accounts and the new Learning and Skills Councils are helping to create the infrastructure that will enable everyone to learn throughout life.

Creating a true Learning Society will depend on equipping all young people with the basic skills of literacy and numeracy, as well as an understanding of how to learn and the motivation to do so. In addition to the Literacy and Numeracy Strategies, we are implementing a new initiative to promote thinking skills in schools and supporting a range of measures to broaden the curriculum and offer wider learning activities (including out-of-school hours) through which young people can learn how to learn. Equally, we are working from the other end of the system to involve parents in Family Learning and other activities which can re-ignite their love of learning and help them offer positive learning role models to young people.

Only by linking our work in schools and lifelong learning in these ways can we create a true Learning Age. I welcome the Campaign for Learning's work in bringing together this collection of essays from some of the UK's foremost thinkers and practitioners as well as its parallel Learning to Learn project, which is exploring how some of the ideas outlined in this book can be applied in today's classrooms to both raise standards and develop true lifelong learners. I look forward to working with them and others to ensure that this becomes possible for all.

Introduction

Bill Lucas and Toby Greany

PUPILS, TEACHERS AND SCHOOLS HAVE achieved much over the last few years and should be justly proud of this. New ideas are being developed which suggest ways in which the role of schools might change in future, whether at the level of classroom practice or in terms of national structures.

Yet schools as we know them are fast becoming an anachronism. They evolved in an agrarian society educating pupils for a factory age, but now find themselves in a new millennium in which patterns of work and learning are changing at an extraordinary speed. Of course schools have changed and developed considerably over the centuries, but despite the best efforts of many wonderful teachers, their very traditions and structures mean that they are educating young people for a world which no longer exists.

Even the words we use, such as 'learn', 'teach', 'school', 'educate', 'train', 'wisdom', 'knowledge' and 'information', have become muddled. 'Teach' is confused with 'learn' and 'knowledge' with 'information'. Interestingly, as an indicator of how change is already overtaking traditional structures, there are now almost as many 'learning centres' in businesses, libraries and community centres as there are schools. In today's turbulent, complex and fast changing society we are on the edge of a paradigm shift which schools, like the language we use about them, are not currently set up to deal with. These are more revolutionary than evolutionary times.

For the past four years we have been moving down two parallel tracks: the tightly defined road towards school improvement and the equally important but less well-mapped series of tracks called lifelong learning. This book brings together some of the country's most eminent thinkers and practitioners to engage in a national debate about how we might allow these two routes to join up more effectively. It seeks, for the first time, to have a serious debate about the most appropriate role for schools in the Learning Age.

In this introduction we start by sketching out our blueprint for a new National Strategy for Learning. We then move on to draw out some of the implications of the contributions to this book. We conclude with our own ideas of how we might do things differently. The Campaign for Learning does not suggest for a moment that it has all, or even many, of the answers. But we are determined to play a part in ensuring that we have a serious discussion about the role of schools. Where we may seem critical of schools we are referring to them as institutions and not to the many excellent people who work and learn in them.

A National Strategy for Learning

An intense debate has been underway for some years in many of the Pacific Rim countries on how the goals and approach of their education systems can promote the skills and attitudes needed for the Learning Age.

Despite initiatives such as the National Commission on Education[1] nearly a decade ago, the UK has been reluctant to adopt a holistic, long-term approach to the learning needs of all of its people.

If we want to look creatively at reforming schools we need to consider how they will fit with the new landscape that is already being sculpted around us today. To do this, we argue that what is needed urgently is a new National Strategy for Learning, covering all stages of our lives as learners and not just the key stages of the time we spend at school.

A National Strategy for Learning would bring together many of the exciting initiatives developed over the last few years and unite them with a view of learning which is truly cradle to grave. It would be driven by a very broad definition of learning, something like the one developed by the Campaign for Learning, which states that:

"Learning is a process of active engagement with experience that may involve an increase in skills, knowledge, understanding, a deepening of values or the capacity to reflect. Effective learning leads to change, development and a desire to learn more." [2]

The Campaign's definition has already been commended by two key thinkers on lifelong learning, Bob Fryer in *Learning for the twenty-first century: first report of the National Advisory Group for Continuing Education and Lifelong Learning*[3] and David Anderson in his influential study of museum education, *Our Commonwealth: museums in the Learning Age*[4].

There is more work to be done on the definition, but at least it shows the breadth of our thinking. It underpins a conception of learning into which, we believe, schools and other institutions need to fit.

A National Strategy would argue a more compelling case for learning than we have so far been offered. It would use a language adapted to the languages of the many different groups that need to be persuaded. It would reach out to teachers, politicians, business people from all sectors, the voluntary sector, community groups, and, of course, the very individuals at the heart of the learning revolution.

A National Strategy would certainly not be starting from scratch. The early sections of *The Learning Age*[5], especially David Blunkett's personal Foreword, contain much that is lyrically persuasive. The Department for Education and Employment's (DfEE's) own current objective,

> *"that all young people reach 16 with the skills, attitudes and personal qualities that will give them a secure foundation for lifelong learning, work and citizenship in a rapidly changing world,"* [6]

is extremely helpful. Equally, *Skills for All*,[7] puts the creation of a culture of lifelong learning as one of the primary recommendations of the National Skills Task Force.

But the truth is that we are, as yet, planning for education and skills, not learning and portfolio lives. And the architects of the current thinking tend to sit in different buildings envisaging different landscapes as they think up their strategies. We have no doubt that, under the current Government, we have made enormous progress on many fronts: but it is now time to urge all those thinking about these issues to come together, listen and work together.

Issues for a National Strategy

If we decided, as a country, to create a Strategy, we would need to consider many issues, just some of which we present here as questions.

What should the government's own strategy for learning be? How might the Department for Trade and Industry's strategy compare with, say, that of the Department of Culture, Media and Support or the Department of Health? Should there be a Ministry for Lifelong Learning? Indeed, would it be helpful to have a Minister whose role is to connect the government's own thinking on learning, possibly modelled on the idea of the Green Minister which now forms a part of the government's approach to sustainable development?

What co-ordinated measures could be taken to create a culture of lifelong learning? Can government change culture or will market forces, especially e-learning and digital television, be more potent mechanisms? How can the current organisational and conceptual divide between pre and post 16 learning be broken down? What is the role of promotion? What demand side measures need to be in place? How do regional and local dimensions need to be explored?

Is it agreed that there are new attitudes, skills and knowledge required to thrive in today's world and, if so, what are they? Is it important that, as a nation, we know more about how our minds work? Is learning to learn a key skill or attribute for each person to acquire and, if so, how is this to be achieved? How can we develop a new pedagogy of lifelong learning that can equip all young people to thrive as independent learners? How should the role of teachers, lecturers and tutors evolve? How much

content should be prescribed or suggested at key life stages and within key sectors? What is the real potential of e-learning? How much of our learning should be 'just in case' and how much 'just in time'?

How can the new breed of 'learning intermediaries' contribute, for example, teaching assistants, personal advisers, learning centre staff, coaches and mentors? Should schools remain connected to local authorities, or might it be time to create new Learning Zones to bring together suppliers of formal and informal learning in greater harmony? How can the new system be made inclusive while maintaining the need for high standards for all? What should be the criteria for inspecting and evaluating schools? How can schools best be supported and encouraged to learn from other sectors? What role should the private sector play? What about parents? And what role the voluntary sector?

To what extent can the current assessment systems be adapted to meet new needs, or do they need radical rethinking?

Is it possible to create a national funding framework for all kinds of learning throughout people's lives, possibly modelled on the approach exemplified by Individual Learning Accounts? Should investment in early and later year's learning be further increased? How would this be paid for?

Thinking about these kinds of questions needs to reflect not only the current reality of schools and the many excellent initiatives underway, but, more fundamentally, the inescapable implications of the lifelong learning revolution that schools must change to keep up with.

Why lifelong learning?

Lifelong learning has emerged relatively recently as a policy area for governments world-wide.

The clearest and simplest argument for life-long learning is stated by Christopher Ball at the start of his chapter: learning pays, for individuals, businesses and nations. This is true more than ever in the 'new' global economy. Capital can now be shifted around the world overnight if cheaper labour or greater efficiency suggests that profits can be enhanced. At the same time, the endless new possibilities opened up by technological innovation allow for customers to be satisfied in ever changing and ever more rapid ways. Because of these changes the capacity to innovate is highly prized and the new capital is human capital. Creativity, teamwork, adaptability innovation and the capacity to manage change are the keys to success.

In response, the early pioneers of the new economy, such as those described by Tom Bentley in his chapter, are creating learning opportunities and cultures well beyond the horizons of the school system: from corporate 'universities' and employee development schemes, to e-learning, action learning sets and a host of other approaches. Other organisations, failing to recognise the potential latent within their own people, are busy fighting a costly war to attract and retain their best talent, at the same time as berating the school system for not producing more of it. Interestingly, as employees themselves recognise the power and importance of learning in this climate, they are increasingly motivated by learning itself as a key component of any workplace benefits package.

The economic case for lifelong learning at the level of the individual and the nation is equally powerful. A woman will earn half a million pounds more during her lifetime if she completes her education, while 60% of people in prison are functionally illiterate or innumerate. At the national level, the final report of the National Skills Task Force[8] outlined some of the most comprehensive research to date for why the UK should invest in raising vocational qualification levels to put us on a par with Germany and so close the productivity gap between the two nations.

There are equally powerful social, cultural, political, moral, health, environmental and technological cases for lifelong learning which have been well rehearsed elsewhere, but can best be understood in the context of changes taking place in society round us.

Post-modern society is a complex and confusing place where we are constantly faced by difficult issues and choices. Cold War and class based verities have broken down, traditional family structures are becoming more fluid, society is increasingly diverse. We define ourselves today not just according to class, political beliefs or geographical location, but according to a shifting set of identities that might include anything from our race, gender, sexuality or religious beliefs, to our shopping or television watching preferences. The old 'brands' are disappearing: careers, banks, churches, shopping centres, universities and, in a sense, schools.

All this indicates why learning is becoming increasingly central to our lives. We need to learn effectively, not just to manage change, but to take control of it. Such learning might be formal, for example gaining a qualification in order to remain employable, to engage in voluntary work, or to fulfill our interests. Or it might be informal; learning to use the Internet to find out about a medical condition or learning to cook Thai food as a pleasurable way to relax. Whatever it is, such learning connects with our deepest needs and desires as individuals and contributes to our engagement with, and understanding of, our wider society. It enables us to realise our potential.

The scale of the challenge

In his chapter Guy Claxton quotes the 1997 Industrial Society report *Speaking Up, Speaking Out*,[9] which was based on interviews with 3,500 11–25 year-olds in the year that new Labour came to power. It concluded that: "Schools are seen as failing to equip young people with the ability to learn for life, rather than for exams". Indeed, Claxton paints a picture of the school as an institution on its last legs.

Sadly, three years into the current reforms, statistics from the Campaign's recent MORI survey[10] of school pupil's attitudes to learning makes depressing reading and suggest that students still find lessons are dominated by copying from the board or a book and listening to the teacher talk for a long time. It is hardly surprising, then, that Michelle Paule describes in her chapter how she continues to see pupils at her school who,

> *"do not perceive themselves as learners, have little experience of success in learning processes, and tend to be characterised by over-dependence on their teachers, resisting taking responsibility for their own learning, and becoming anxious or uncooperative".*

Putting schools at the heart of the Learning Age

The DfEE has implemented many excellent policies aimed at developing the UK's lifelong learning potential over the past few years. But, as the majority of the contributors to this book argue, the two functions of schooling and lifelong learning remain a long way apart. A symptom of this can be seen in Chris Woodhead, Her Majesty's Chief Inspector of Schools, who in his Annual Lecture in 2000[11], questioned the legitimacy of the aspirations of those who believe in lifelong learning. Specifically, he doubted that it is sensible for plumbers to aspire to higher education, and went on to challenge whether concepts like lifelong learning and learning to learn are meaningful.

In his chapter, Michael Barber outlines the Government's exhaustive pre-16 policy focussed on raising standards for all. He is rightly proud of initiatives such as the Literacy and Numeracy strategies, Excellence in Cities, the approach to teachers' continuing professional development and the out of school hours learning described by Mike Walton and Kay Andrews in their chapter. Equally, he might have referred to the Curriculum 2000 reforms, the thinking skills pilot projects now underway in some authorities or the initiatives being developed in the wake of the Social Exclusion Unit's excellent *Schools Plus*[12] report. Barber's undoubted enthusiasm and recognition of true learning displays itself in his comment that,

> *"the most heartening evidence so far of the impact of the strategy is not last year's test scores, but the fact that teachers and heads can see the difference day-to-day in the capacity of their pupils".*

We applaud the fact that examination results have risen steadily since 1997. Examinations remain a key stamp on an individual's passport to further or higher education, successful employment and self-esteem. Few people would advocate rejecting examinations as a key measure of success. The important question, however, is whether they should be the only serious measure of learning. We need to work out the sensible relationship between examinations and intrinsic motivation. We need to be clearer about how we assess the creativity, resilience, resourcefulness and reflexiveness which are at the heart of being an effective lifelong learner.

This takes us to the real issues of how we learn and how this can be measured. It is what Titus Alexander refers to in his chapter as "an acute tension at the centre of government education policy". The best learning, he writes, echoing John Abbott, Terry Ryan and Guy Claxton's analysis, is about people thinking for themselves, following their curiosity, discovering new things, and developing competence with words, numbers, books, science, technology and people as they do so.

Michelle Paule still finds that school leavers are ill prepared for lifelong learning. She suggests that the sheer weight of content in the current curriculum model inhibits learning by restricting the range and creativity of classroom experiences; leaving too many students engaged in accumulating information, which they cannot see the use of beyond school, in order to pass tests and examinations.

She, along with the other practising teacher in this collection, Tony Hinkley, sees the challenge for the school of the future as being about adopting a much more coherent approach to developing meta-cognitive processes, in understanding how we learn. Encouragingly, she describes how signposts to this road are already being put in place through the Gifted and Talented programme.

From schools to community centres for lifelong learning

All of the contributors to this book think that schools should do things differently. In their different ways they suggest how schools could play new roles, more fitting for the world in which they find themselves.

Nevertheless, despite this apparent consensus, the question that remains is a difficult one. How much change can be accommodated within our existing deeply entrenched cultural understanding of what schools do?

Much will depend on the lead taken by government in initiating a national debate on the role of schools, one in which it lays out a clear vision of how and why they should change. We describe here our view of what that vision might be. A vision which, we believe, should form part of the National Strategy advocated above.

In line with contributors such as Bob Fryer, Phil Street and Tony Hinkley, we believe that schools can only become the powerhouses of lifelong learning that they must be if they are transformed into community centres for lifelong learning. Building on the best examples of community schools and on the full school movement in America and Scotland, they would bring together integrated provision of a range public services on one site, engaging the full resources of communities to offer learning for the real world.

These community centres would be far more supple and responsive to the needs of their communities and of individual learners than is currently the case. In this sense they would take the current moves towards specialist schools and the focus on the needs of specific groups, such as gifted and talented students, a stage further. Rather than being driven solely by the needs of young people, they would be centres for parents and other adults to continue their own learning and would draw extensively on other resources for learning within the community, including local employers, along the lines suggested by Tom Bewick in his chapter.

The centres would operate according to Knowledge rather than Agrarian Age principles, opening throughout the year, for more hours of the day and at weekends. They would be responsible for developing provision for all age groups, and so would simultaneously be encouraging families to learn together, providing work-based learning and placements with employers, and managing children's learning processes. They would be equipped to support multiple modes of learning, including e-learning and online delivery, apprenticeship learning, project-based learning in the community and home schooling. The centres would be able to meet the needs of the emerging e-generations described by Stephen Heppell. They could, for example, manage community learning grids to connect learning groups, through closed intranets, in a network from people's digital TV screens at home to the centre's server and beyond.

The centres would support effective learning in the early years by working with parents and other services from before birth to ensure the best possible development at this crucial stage. Far from 'hot-housing' young children, they would focus on developing the positive dispositions required for learning, including self esteem, confidence and motivation. While the adult to child ratio at this early stage would allow for intensive support, older children would be encouraged to take responsibility for their own learning and would work with children of varying ages, rather than in set chronological year groups. Rather than being assessed at a certain age, they would be involved in on-going formative assessment.

New views of intelligence and learning

These changes would reflect a new vision and culture of schooling, one that is based on lifelong learning, rather than on school or college. Central to this would be a view of intelligence as something that is multi-faceted and latent in every individual, and of learning as something that must, first and foremost, engage and develop the individual in the way that the Campaign's definition above suggests.

Whilst ensuring that all young people are equipped with the basic skills of literacy and numeracy, the task of the teacher would be as a learning 'manager', equipping them with the basic skill of 'learnacy' or learning to learn. This would be through an explicit focus on the skill of learning to learn, giving pupils structured opportunities to explore the cognitive processes involved in learning and helping them understand their own particular blend of intelligence and learning style and how they should develop these. Ultimately, all students should be able to transfer and apply this 'learnacy' to new areas and issues as they arise throughout life. Motivation would be key here, and would be enhanced by giving learners increasing amounts of control over their learning and by making clear the connections between the learning in different parts of their lives.

Clearly, this model implies major changes to the current curriculum and means of assessing learning in schools. In his chapter, Tom Bentley proposes that the current curriculum be halved in order to free up time for learning. Elsewhere, Valerie Bayliss at the RSA has argued that we need a competence based, rather than knowledge based, curriculum and has begun to explore what this might mean in practice.[13] We would certainly agree with these proposals, particularly Bayliss' recognition that skills and attitudes should replace knowledge as the foremost outcome for education, although we would go further to argue that understanding how to learn, the creativity advocated by Ken Robinson and Tom Bentley, and what Guy Claxton calls 'the new 3 Rs' of resilience, resoucefulness and reflectiveness should also be key outcomes.

Ultimately, the rationale underpinning the new centres could best be summed up by John Holt, writing in the last century:

"Since we cannot know what knowledge will be most needed in the future, it is senseless to try to teach it in advance. Instead, we should try to turn out people who love learning so much and learn so well that they will be able to learn whatever needs to be learned". [14]

Managing and assessing the new forms of learning

How might these lifelong learning competencies and dispositions best be taught? Clearly, there is much excellent practice already on offer in schools to learn from.

For example, the Literacy and Numeracy strategies have given many teachers a better understanding of how skills can be taught explicitly, and the Literacy Strategy is now showing how this can be done across different curriculum areas at Key Stage 3. Equally, the schools involved in the Campaign's Learning to Learn action research project are exploring how this key skill can be developed and how an understanding of the brain and how we learn impacts on their own teaching.

Another, equally important, question is how this new lifelong learning curriculum might best be assessed? One thing seems certain, the dominance of the current examination methodology would need to be reduced. Examinations as we know them are not a very effective means of assessing the new lifelong learning competencies. Project-based assessment and the accreditation of learning in a wider range of spheres could easily replace some examinations, while the DfEE's work on the Progress File and the assessment of key skills could form the basis for assessing learning dispositions and competencies.

What might an individual pupil experience and what roles would he or she be expected to play in this brave new learning world? As John Abbott argues in his chapter and Professor David Hargreaves has argued elsewhere[15], we appear to be programmed to learn best through apprenticeship. This implies more than simply having an expert mentor to watch and learn from, but also that our learning is relevant and contextualised and that it leads to autonomous competence. This is by no means to say that all learning must be vocational, but rather that learners must learn from and with a range of community mentors, completing tasks and fulfilling roles that the learners themselves have helped define.

Equally, fulfilling the adage that the best way to learn is to teach, learners will increasingly be responsible for helping others to learn. At its simplest, the proposed system would give increasing freedom to learners as they proved that they were ready for this. They could utilise the learning centre's resources, often working with other learners, to complete projects agreed with their teachers under varying degrees of supervision. Ultimately, the aim would be for learners to become responsible for managing their own learning; recognising how they learn, able to learn from mistakes and constantly seeking to expand and develop themselves.

New roles for teachers

The role of teachers would clearly need to be transformed, so that they become the managers, not arbiters, of learning. Rather than being experts in particular subject areas they would, first and foremost, be experts in helping young people understand how they learn and in supporting them to do so. To achieve this they would need to liase with a range of other agencies, with their role being as the final guardian of the young learner's interests and assessor of his or her learning achievements and needs.

In this sense they could usefully be compared to the new mentors being developed through the Connexions strategy. The analogy is apt because it highlights the principles of inclusivity and connective pedagogy outlined by Martin Stephenson in his chapter. Too many pupils are currently excluded from schools and almost all feel that they are not connected to the complex society they must enter. The new system must not become a sink or swim environment in which some thrive, some drift and others are left to drown. Teachers must have the expertise and support structures in place to work with all students in the most appropriate manner.

While all teachers would be responsible for developing learners' basic and key skills, subject specialists would still be needed to provide learning programmes for those with particular interests and needs. Others would cater for sex education, careers counselling and other essential areas. In this sense, the approach might be seen as a radical extension of the French Baccaulauriat system, but with greater choice for the learner and a stronger recognition that not all learning happens in classrooms.

One of the prime implications of these changes is that teachers themselves must become role models as learners. To do this they need much greater scope for professional development in the world for which they are preparing young people. This might be achieved through a new kind of competence insurance, linked to a national sabbatical programme like the one described by Anne Evans in her chapter. Or it might be a more radical approach that encourages teachers to work part-time or to move in and out of teaching throughout their life. It will also be important that teachers are skilled at helping adults as well as children to learn, so that they can engage parents and others in supporting the learning process to best effect. Such a highly complex and responsible role would need to remunerated and valued accordingly.

Considerable schools-based training is now a part of all initial teacher training courses. This development could be extended so that some schools also become higher education centres, with a research capacity. They would be centres for action research and play a local role in encouraging reflective practice and co-ordinating mentoring.

New learning intermediaries

Teachers will need to be supported in their role by a far more comprehensive set of learning intermediaries and support workers than at present. These would include community mentors in workplaces and the range of other organisations in which young learners might spend time completing agreed projects, as well as specialist coaches experienced in leading particular learning projects, ranging from on-line collaborative research to outward bound activities. Retired people could certainly be engaged in supporting this process more effectively than at present, while the recent *Manifesto for Family Learning*[16], published by the Campaign and others, suggests that parents could be encouraged and supported to have time off work in schools supporting learning.

Equally important will be a new breed of classroom assistants, capable of supporting teachers in the dynamic and diverse classrooms of the future. In addition to providing administrative support, freeing up teachers to focus on learning, these learning assistants would work with individual pupils and small groups to monitor and assist their learning, feeding information back to the teacher and ensuring that individuals do not get 'lost' in the new, more complex, environment. The Campaign has already begun to explore, with the DfEE, Southampton University and Select Education, the skills needed for this and other similar professions that could be developed through a new Centre for the Learning Assistant.

Wider issues

A whole raft of issues concerning how the new centres should be structured and governed will need to be explored in detail and resolved. Pay structures will certainly need to be reformed to reflect and reward teachers' new roles, while systems for rewarding mentors and for parents tithing their time will need to be established. At the governance level, there is certainly a case for reforming the current system of school governors, to move towards a more professionalised management system.

In parallel with the development of schools' role, there is the opportunity for the architecture and design connections with the past to be broken once and for all. Schools no longer need to look like prison yards or municipal buildings. As the charity Learning through Landscapes has demonstrated, the quality of the environment has a profound effect on learning. Crucially, the involvement of all site users in the design process will be critically important to the success of this development.

At a local level, the role of local authorities is already changing, as described by Tony Breslin, and this process should arguably continue so that schools are guaranteed sound administrative support, funding that reflects their needs based on a national formula and high quality opportunities for training and development. All these might be better provided through local or regional Learning Zones that also manage the process of linking employers and other organisations with schools along the lines suggested by Tom Bewick. In addition to overseeing the funding of learning opportunities for young people and professional development placements for teachers, these could oversee overarching roles, such as admissions and special needs provision. In many ways these roles concord with the Local Government Association's own view of the future of the LEA in 2020, which it sees as being defined "not by the services it provides to schools, but by its ability to help children and families access learning to suit their individual needs".[17]

Finally, the role of quality assurance and data collection needs further scrutiny.

What Ofsted does and how it operates would certainly need to be rethought, not only in terms of the criteria it uses for judging schools, but also with regard to its relation to central government.

We need a National Strategy for Learning that creates a seamless system of provision in which schools, as community centres for lifelong learning, play a dynamic and important role.

[1] *Learning to succeed: a radical look at education today and a strategy for the future*, Paul Hamlyn Foundation, 1993
[2] *Learning to Live*, Campaign for Learning, 1997
[3] *Learning for the twenty-first century: first report of the National Advisory Group for Continuing Education and Lifelong Learning*, 1997
[4] David Anderson, *Our Commonwealth: museums in the Learning Age*, Museums Association, 1999
[5] *The Learning Age*, Department for Education and Employment, 1998
[6] DfEE Objective 1, *Learning and working together for the future*, DfEE, 1998
[7] *Skills for all: Proposals for a National Skills Agenda*, Final Report of the National Skills Task Force, 2000
[8] *Skills for all: Research Report*, Final Report of the National Skills Task Force, 2000
[9] *Speaking up, speaking out*, Research Report, Industrial Society, 1997
[10] Bill Lucas and Toby Greany, *Learning to Learn: setting the agenda for schools in the twenty-first century*, Campaign for Learning/Network Educational Press, 2000
[11] Chris Woodhead speaking at the Annual HMCI lecture, RSA, 2000
[12] *Schools Plus*, Social Exclusion Unit/Cabinet Office, 2000
[13] Valerie Bayliss, *Opening Minds*, RSA, 1999
[14] John Holt, *How children learn*, Penguin 1965
[15] David Hargreaves, *Future of Britain*, ESRC Social Science Conference, 1997
[16] *A Manifesto for Family Learning*, Campaign for Learning, 2000
[17] *Education in 2020*, LGA education discussion paper, 2000

Motivation and readiness to learn

Christopher Ball

IF LEARNING PAYS, WHY AREN'T WE ALL KEENER to do it? This paradox is my point of departure. It is as if, knowing that bread is nourishing and stones are not, many people preferred stones to bread for breakfast. Or, being aware that fire burns, they repeatedly stretched their hands into the flames. Of course, some do behave in this way. The proportion of 11–15 year olds who smoke regularly rose from 10% to 13% between 1990 and 1996. I believe that behaviour like this is rooted in low self-esteem. And resistance to learning has the same cause.

The assertion that learning pays is a commonplace today. Successful learning enhances both life and work. It is the source of health, wealth and happiness. It benefits individuals, organisations and communities. Does this general truth require further proof? In a recent study of the city of Derby it was found that average earnings were higher, and unemployment lower, among those with degrees (level 4) than those with A-levels or (G)NVQ (level 3), and that the same relationship held between level 3 and level 2 (GCSE), and most markedly between level 2 and those with no qualifications at all.[1]

Many such studies have demonstrated the link between higher levels of formal educational qualifications and economic success for individuals. More interesting, perhaps, is the evidence that prolonged initial education, to level 3 or 4 or beyond, seems to correlate with the deferred onset of senile decay, as does the active exercise of the brain in old age. I have no doubt that the practice of learning should be added to a healthy diet, sensible exercise and the avoidance of smoking, drugs and stress as the basic prescription for a good life.

So why don't people practise learning with the same enthusiasm they bring to holidays, sport or mealtimes? "Learning sucks", said Craig, aged 15, in response to a survey of attitudes to learning in 1996 carried out by the Campaign for Learning, "I hate school".[2] About 1 in 6 people reject formal education. 16% of adults and school-leavers say that they hated school. Almost 1 in 6 school-children disrupt their classes, or go AWOL, or, as I often did, play truant by withdrawing into their own thoughts, or are excluded. Not surprisingly, 20% of adults have poor numeracy skills – and 15% of adults and school-leavers have poor literacy skills. If we weren't used to it, we would surely find the high failure rate of formal education astonishing. Why does it happen?

Why people fail to learn

I believe that there are four (and only four) reasons why people fail to learn. They are, in order of importance: low self-esteem and lack of confidence; weak motivation; insufficient ability or potential and lack of opportunities. It is true that in the past many people have been deprived of the opportunity to learn. One obvious example is the long struggle of women to achieve equality of opportunity for entry to higher education. But such battles have been substantially won. As we start the 21st century, the UK is able to offer everyone in principle, and also by and large in practice, two years of pre-school education, eleven years of full-time, compulsory and free schooling, free post-school education to the age of 18, and entry to higher education for at least a third of the age cohort. Lack of opportunity is not the major problem today.

Nor is lack of ability. In any large population we may expect some 3% to have severe learning difficulties, a further 20% or so to have mild learning difficulties, and the rest to be 'normal learners'. No one disputes that the 3% needs, and should get, special care and support: and on the whole they do. Given enough time and appropriate support the 20% can achieve the same levels of learning as the 'normal learners'. Human ability is not in short supply. We are nearly all potentially high achievers, or (at least) we were at the beginning of our lives.

I am interested in the idea that people can, and should learn how to learn more effectively. Learning is instinctive: all humans are naturally adept at informal learning. But formal learning is a different matter. Most of us could do with help in making the best use of our opportunities for formal learning in school, college or university. Some need strategies to help them survive or tolerate the experience.

What about informal learning? Although the instinct to learn is as innate and natural as the instinct to breathe, athletes, singers and asthmatics can all benefit from the help and advice of a good 'breathing coach'. 'Learning coaches' seem to me to be one of the missing links of the education and training services. I would happily invest time and money in a coach who could help me learn faster. But I already know that the first step towards faster learning is the enhancement of self-esteem and confidence and the intensification of motivation, not just wanting, but really wanting, to learn.

This essay is about motivation and readiness to learn, not ability or opportunity. But before addressing these very real problems I want to state as plainly as I can my belief that an obsession with the issues of opportunity and ability has distracted the attention of education and society for too long from what really needs to be considered, namely low self-esteem and lack of confidence, and weak motivation, the first two reasons why people fail to learn.

Being ready to learn

My thesis is that the combination of high self-esteem, confidence and strong motivation normally provides a sufficient condition for successful learning; and that the first two (self-esteem and confidence) are a necessary, but not sufficient, condition for motivation. The first task for educators, therefore, and for those who support learners is to build up people's self-esteem and confidence so that they become 'ready to learn'. The second is to help people to strengthen their own motivation. How is this to be done?

Rats and babies seem to thrive when they are well fed, exercised, loved, stimulated and comfortable. No surprises there. Children and adults alike need nourishment, exercise, companionship, stimulation and a good home. Such conditions encourage the brain to develop and switch on the learning instinct. They also promote self-esteem and confidence. So if you want to become a successful learner, eat well, take plenty of exercise, surround yourself with loving companions, stimulate your brain and dwell in a congenial environment. And help others to do likewise.

High achievers are, typically, good learners with boundless self-esteem and confidence. They love being themselves and believe that they can master anything they set their hands or minds to. They are usually right. What marks them out from ordinary people are three key conditions which obtained during their formative years – plenty of 'warm, demanding adults', an exploratory curriculum of learning, and only limited access to their peer group. While not forgetting the importance of nourishment, exercise and the environment, I think it is the combination of love and stimulation represented in this formula that is so vital to successful learning. Not only children, but adults also, need to surround themselves with 'warm, demanding adults' – parents and grandparents, elder siblings, mentors, tutors, coaches and friends. Choose your own support team and cherish them: they will give you the inestimable benefit of self-esteem and confidence, 'readiness to learn'. This is the critical first step towards learning success and high achievement.

That love makes the world go round is not a new thought. 'Learn to love and leave all other' advised Holy Church in Langland's great poem, Piers Plowman, offering an early and delightfully simple sketch for a national curriculum.[3] She was right. I doubt whether anyone would question the recommendation that learning feeds on love, and that learners, ourselves included, need love to thrive and succeed. Self-esteem is proper love of oneself: it is engendered by the love of others.

Stimulation is more complicated. The brain is switched on and switched off by stress. I like to distinguish between 'good stress' and 'bad stress', challenge and threat. People learn best in an environment of high challenge and low threat. Indeed, as the following matrix suggests, the response of learners to different combinations of challenge and threat is critically important.

	High Challenge	Low Challenge
High Threat	Anxious	Dim
Low Threat	Bright	Spoilt

If you want people to be bright, lively, intelligent, responsive learners, provide them with an environment characterised by high levels of challenge coupled with low levels of threat. Children's play or adult sports typically demonstrate this combination. That is why they are such fun. If we want people to learn, we need to provide a comparable learning environment with the right kind of stimulation.

Readiness to learn is no mystery. It consists of confidence and self-esteem, and these qualities develop naturally in people whose lives are rich in love and challenge. Provided they are not demotivated by rigidly imposed curriculums of learning, or 'dumbed down' by overexposure to the peer group, they will be successful learners with every chance of developing into high achievers.

The nature of successful learning

The reason why the imposed curriculum is a deterrent to some learners is that motivation and readiness to learn usually require the five Cs: choice, challenge, clarity, confidence and comfort. With all these in place successful learning is likely. As you progressively reduce the five Cs, you increase the probability of failure. Choice is critical.

Beware of the peer group! William Golding's *The Lord of the Flies* shows what I mean.[4] The worst excesses of English football supporters are a case in point. Peer-group pressure dumbs you down. By the peer-group I mean people of one's own age and kind. There is a sad truth in human nature that all segregation tends to be harmful and complete segregation is completely disastrous. This rule can be observed in operation whenever people are segregated by race, religion, gender, age – or any other discriminator. We thrive on diversity, not segregation.

Believing this, I am growing more and more uneasy with the 'school-and-classroom' model of traditional formal education. It fails all three tests of the formula of

"plenty of warm, demanding adults, an exploratory curriculum of learning, and only limited access to the peer-group".

Home schooling seems nearer the ideal. Not surprisingly, it appears to be remarkably successful. Though growing fast, home schooling is unlikely to provide a panacea in current social conditions. For those whose confidence and self-esteem have been damaged, and whose motivation is at a low ebb, developmental education, offered by organisations such as the Landmark Forum, can make a real difference.

I wrote earlier that self-esteem and confidence are a necessary, but not sufficient, condition for motivation. Let me give an example. I cannot drive, not through lack of opportunity or ability (or so I believe!), but because I do not want to. I have never had driving lessons and never will. But I am not short of self-esteem and confidence. Could some brilliant teacher motivate me to learn? I do not think so.

Motivation comes from within. Others can tempt, persuade or inspire us (or advertisements would not work!), but we retain our freedom to choose or reject what is offered. If you want to learn about motivation, study marketing. It is a powerful and effective discipline, and some of those who practise it are brilliantly successful. But even the brothers Saatchi cannot sell anything to anyone. I am glad of that. I value free will, idiosyncratic choice and personal difference. I would be sorry if advertisers or governments or gurus or teachers ever found the secret of motivating others to do their bidding. But that will not happen: there is no secret. Motivation comes from within. Of course, if the question is how to motivate oneself, the answer is simple – increase your confidence and self-esteem. Go back to the beginning of this essay and read it again!

[1] *Learning Pays...for Derby,* Policy Research Institute Leeds Metropolitan University, 1996

[2] *Attitudes to Learning,* Campaign for Learning, London, 1996

[3] William Langland, *Piers Plowman,* W.W. Norton & Co. Inc, 1990

[4] William Golding, *Lord of the Flies,* Faber and Faber, 1997

What would schools be like if they were truly dedicated to helping all young people become confident, competent lifelong learners?

Guy Claxton

"Doubt is an uncomfortable condition, but certainty is a ridiculous one". Voltaire

THE GREAT GALLEON OF STATE EDUCATION IS becalmed, and its crew are frantically busy varnishing the decks and remaking the beds in a vain attempt to get it going again. On the bridge endless seminars are held, and schemes hatched, yet even this amount of hot air is unable to fill the slack canvas. Having been deliberately driven into the lee, the boat will not move again until it ventures out of its protected anchorage, and dares to fill its sails with the wind of change.

Vital signs

There are four signals of the failure of education, of the depth of failure. One: young people know that schools are not equipping them to face the complex demands and uncertainties of the future, or even of the present. Based on interviews with 3,500 11–25 year-olds, the Industrial Society report *Speaking Up, Speaking Out* concludes:

"Most young people fear that their world will generally become more challenging, and some have a bleak view of future opportunities and trends... Their lives are riddled with insecurity... Insecurity becomes an integral part of growing up... Schools are seen as failing to equip young people with the ability to learn for life, rather than for exams".[1]

Two: the vast majority of adults involved in any way with education know the same thing. Every time I give a talk now, I carry out a straw poll. I ask the audience whether they think that: a) schools are doing a good job of equipping most young people for the future; b) they would be, if all the currently mooted reforms were implemented successfully; or c) we have got a long way to go.

Out of about 1600 informants, including teachers from early childhood to higher education, governors, advisors, inspectors and parents, I have had three votes for a), 36 for b), and the rest for c). On closer questioning, the overwhelming majority accept that it is the model of education that needs to change. It is not just 'poverty' or 'home background' or 'leadership' or 'pay'.

Three: the low level of confidence, qualification, literacy and numeracy amongst 20% or more of school-leavers does not just show that school has failed to give them what they need. It has left many of them with the belief that they cannot learn; they are unable to repair for themselves the holes that were left by school. They are not just relatively illiterate and innumerate; they are 'illearner-ate' too. One 18-year-old brickie in the Industrial Society report said: "Say I got laid off, I've got nothing, nothing to help me get another job... I've got no other skill." An education system that leaves young people with so little confidence in their ability to learn is not fit for the 21st century.

Four: even the relative successes of school are not necessarily good at real-life learning. In one study a group of 13 year-old girls were given a booklet of maths problems, in the middle of which were some questions that were too hard for all the girls, even the high achievers, to do. On the problems after the too-difficult ones, many of these high achieving girls did worse even than their lower-achieving peers. They had gone to pieces. Their performance overall is good, but their confidence, their "stickability", their resilience in the face of difficulty and frustration is shallow and brittle.[2] And what could be more important for the real-life learner, grappling with all kinds of complexities and uncertainties, than this resilience?

There may also be a Four b): we might also wonder about the effectiveness of a school system, some of the conspicuous successes of which, the people in whose hands the future of education itself now lies, seem to be so woefully lacking in imagination, ingenuity and the ability to grasp the real depth of the problems which their system is facing.

They keep acting as if varnishing and bed-making would be likely to do the trick. People who are unable to acknowledge genuine complexity, and seem incapable of ever saying "I don't know", which is where all learning has to start, are not very good advertisements for lifelong learning.

Education for the Learning Age

We know much more about the mind than we did a hundred years ago, and one of the most important things we know is that learning itself is learnable. We used to think that if a child struggled with their learning, or made mistakes, that meant that they suffered from social deprivation or poor teaching, or they had not tried very hard, or they were not very bright. Now we know that there are a variety of other possible reasons, each of which a teacher can do something about. They might lack confidence in their ability to learn. They might just not have mastered the requisite learning tool yet. Or they might not have realised for themselves that something they do know how to do is relevant. The great Swiss psychologist Jean Piaget once defined intelligence as "knowing what to do when you don't know what to do". When learning is hard, one way of looking at it is as an opportunity to get smarter, in Piaget's terms; or, for a teacher, to help someone else get smarter by coaching or modelling the skill they need.

Education for the Learning Age is about helping people become better 'real-life learners'.[3] Young people want their education to give them a powerful, effective send-off as lifelong learners. They, their parents and their teachers know the world is changing fast, and they know that they cannot be taught in advance what they will need to know — because nobody knows what that will be. Instead, as the great American educator John Holt said, as long ago as the 1960s:

"we should try to turn out people who love learning so much, and who learn so well, that they will be able to learn whatever needs to be learned".[4]

And this means out-of-school, real-life learning; not just the kind that gets you examination passes. For we know that you can be good at school without learning to be good at life – and vice versa.

Schools, spurred on by league tables and the like, can raise their exam results without raising their students' 'learnacy'. A young swimmer can improve her personal best if you loop a rope round her chest and tow her down the pool. But, if you do so, are you helping her become a better swimmer? No. And are you actually undermining the development of her swimming ability? Yes. Just so, teachers can train their students to do better on the tests in such a way that, whether they know it or not, they are weakening rather than strengthening the students' real-life learning power. For example there is evidence that young children who are hothoused, or subjected to overly academic teaching, show long-term deficits as learners that more than offset any short-term gains. Rebecca Marcon, the author of this research explains that:

"later progress is slowed for most children when formal learning experiences are introduced too early. Pushing children too soon into 'formalised academics' can actually backfire when children move into the later childhood grades where they are required to think more independently. This is because

teacher-directed approaches that tell children what to do, when to do it, and how to do it curtail the development of autonomy".[5]

And isn't 'autonomy', the ability to think for yourself and manage your own learning, one of the key abilities of the lifelong learner?

Cognitive science is telling us loud and clear that what we do, as parents and teachers, can significantly raise or lower young people's real-life learning power. And it is telling us that too much preoccupation with raising achievement or attainment can be one very effective way of lowering it. Conversely, if teachers want to, they can see themselves predominantly not as transmitters of bodies of knowledge, skill and understanding, but as learning coaches. This does not mean throwing out the content of the curriculum. Nor does it mean that we should adopt a laissez-faire or ideologically 'child-centred' approach to education. It means that, if we want to help all young people become better real-life learners, we need to shift our priorities. If you want to learn 'hammering', you've got to have some nails to practice on. But the point is not how many nails you have hammered in, nor how beautifully flat they are, but how well you have learned to hammer – especially with new kinds of nails in the context of different kinds of jobs.

Mind gym

As educators we have to learn to shift our attention from the 'Know Zone' to the 'Grow Zone'. The Know Zone is what you have already mastered. It is like an island of competence in the midst of a sea of uncertainty. Expanding the size of this island, especially in some key areas, is important. But it is not as important as helping young people expand the size of their Grow Zone, the coastal region in which they are off-shore and unsure, grappling with the, as yet' unknown and unmastered. Learning to be out of your depth without panicking, to swim, to dive below the surface of the known: these are the core life skills for the 21st century.

In order to help young people to become better learners, the first thing is for all teachers to start thinking, acting and talking as if learning were learnable; and as if children's learning difficulties signalled not a lack of ability, but opportunities to develop their 'learning muscles'. Not everyone is going to become another Michael Owen or Ashia Hansen, but that doesn't mean it is a waste of time going to the gym. We can all develop our physical strength, skill and stamina, and getting hot and sweaty is a good indicator that your exercise is paying off. And so with our minds. If young people saw each lesson as a useful session in the 'mind gym', and could understand how their real-life learning power was being systematically improved, it is a fair bet that they would bunk off, mess about, and deliberately 'go stupid' much less than they do at present.

This point is so important it bears some hammering. If you believed that your physique was genetically determined, then physical exercise would look like a waste of time; and getting hot and sweaty would simply be an unpleasant reminder of your limitations. If we talk to young people as if their minds were similarly of fixed capacity, and as if their successes, failures and difficulties were symptomatic of the size of these general-purpose pots of 'intelligence' or 'ability' (whether you think there are eight such pots, a la Howard Gardner, or only

one) they are going to become averse to learning.[6] As soon as they do not know what to do, they are going to interpret this as showing that they are relatively stupid, and will, as we all do when so threatened, consequently act to protect their self-respect. To have your errors made public, in a classroom where this 'fixed pot' explanation has been regularly used, is to be shamed. Whereas, with a teacher who wants you to learn how to learn, and knows you can, finding things hard, and working through your errors, is quite a different experience individually and socially. There are many classrooms in Hungary and Singapore where children queue up to have their mistakes worked through on the board.

It follows, by the way, that, just as you do not get fitter by lying in bed, so you do not develop your learning skills and stamina by being protected from difficulty. There are those who have assumed that children's 'self-esteem' is best preserved by protecting them from experiences of failure or frustration, and by creating a gently graded curriculum cunningly designed to prevent anyone ever breaking sweat. But as I have explained, it is not difficulty per se that is upsetting; only the attribution of difficulty to a low level of 'ability'. It turns out to be the children who have least experience of grappling with difficulty, and sometimes 'winning', who have the thinnest veneer of resilience.

Being a learning coach
It is perfectly simple for any teacher to create a classroom culture within which 'difficulty' is seen as not just normal but beneficial. First they stop using 'ability' attributions, and start talking as if learning were learnable. Then they make a point of 'celebrating stuckness' just as much as

success. They notice and acknowledge intelligent engagement, and treat difficulties and errors as valuable and noteworthy. They create opportunities for every child to work at the limits of their learning, and expect them to do so. It is coasting that is called into question, not struggling. There are classrooms the ethos of which have been transformed by the teacher simply opening up the question of "what we do when we don't know what to do" for general discussion. Children soon get used to sharing ideas about what to do when you are 'stuck', and enjoy creating posters that summarise this home-grown wisdom, and which act as continual visual prompts and reminders. There are classes where children are so used to spending the last five minutes of a lesson talking about "what I found hard in that activity, and what helped me to move on", and find it so useful, that they remind the teacher if it looks as if they might run out of time. There are classes where children as young as six keep, or are helped to keep, a weekly diary of their 'journey into the unknown', in which they learn how to develop a dialogue with their teacher, through writing, about their own learning strengths and weaknesses, ups and downs, and self-selected learning-to-learn targets.

If effective real-life learners have developed a robust and resilient approach to learning, they have also made sure that they have a good repertoire of learning skills and strategies to call on when they need. They have access to and an interest in all the compartments of the learning tool-kit. And here we have to overcome the second major misconception about learning. It is not homogeneous. There is no one best way of learning everything. And it is certainly untrue that a deliberate, conscious, intellectual approach is always to be striven for and preferred. If Jean Piaget gave us a useful definition of intelligence, he also sold education the singularly unhelpful idea that we grow through, and out of, a succession of 'childish' ways of learning and knowing on our way to the goal, the pinnacle of mental development: abstract, formal, logical reason.

There are four main compartments of the learning toolkit, learning through immersion, through imagination, through intuition and through intellect. The accomplished real-life learner needs them all. Sure, each of these starts to develop at different ages, but they continue to do so, if we let them, throughout life. Infants, for example, learn to attune themselves to the rituals and regularities of their early lives simply by 'immersion'. Their marvellous, self-motivating, self-organising brains pick up the patterns that surround them and spin those patterns into subtle webs of social and practical expertise. No external instruction or deliberate intent is required. And exactly the same faculty will deliver intuitive mastery to the new manager, the new GP and the new parent. Brain-based learning by immersion will generate practical expertise in situations that are too complicated to figure out. Or it will if it has not got neglected, or gummed up by too much thinking. Just looking, and just messing about, without striving for conscious comprehension, are highly intelligent ways of learning. Education for real-life learning must encourage patient attentiveness and playful experimentation, and strengthen young people's ability to tolerate temporary confusion.

Likewise imagination is not a childish way of thinking. Mental rehearsal is a smart tool for developing real-life expertise, and for exploring new ways to act in complicated or stressful situations. Athletes, managers and top scientists know the value of imagination – as they do of intuition, the third compartment. 'Intuition', in this sense, is the ability to let your mind go soft and quiet, and allow things to 'come to you'. Reverie is the nursery of creativity. People who can access a state of reverie voluntarily are more creative than others.[7] Being slow is sometimes smart, and helping people to learn how to make use of what I have called their 'tortoise mind' is part of education for lifelong learning.[8] 'Creativity' is the ability to come up with good ideas in unprecedented situations. Surely there is no more important life skill than that. It is certainly one that employers are crying out for.

Learning coaches make sure that there are opportunities to practice and develop all the tools in the learning toolkit. Observing and experimenting are not the prerogative of the science teacher. Imagination is not the exclusive preserve of the teacher of drama or art. Logical reasoning is not the only learning skill you need in maths. Good science teachers help students learn the scope, the value and limitations of imagination; good maths teachers encourage students to explore and develop their intuition; good art and music teachers teach you how to look and listen. In every lesson, teachers can be asking students what learning strategies they are using, and suggesting other approaches to try, and students can thus be continually extending their sense of what to do when they do not know what to do.

In general, the learning coach is looking for ways of showing students what good learning looks like, and encouraging them to think and talk about their processes of learning, as well as the products. "How did you go about that?" "What worked and what didn't?" "What else could you have tried?" These are the kinds of questions continually on their lips. Young people who have become fluent in the language of learning, who know how to talk to each other about their ups and downs and methods, are less likely to flounder or get upset when the going gets tough.

Examples of learning: shining and warning

And more important even than encouraging students to talk about learning is the teacher's ability, and willingness, to model the thoughts and feelings of a genuine learner. In a committed learning school, teachers are not afraid to be seen to be learners. They do not feel obliged to know everything, all the time. In fact they see it as an essential part of their professional role to model what Harvard psychologist Ellen Langer calls 'confident uncertainty', and to let themselves be seen in the process of learning.[9] English teachers show their students drafts of their own writing, and talk to them, from their own experience, about how hard writing is. Maths teachers work through problems on the board that they do not know the solution to, thinking aloud as they do so. Science teachers have their own experiments set up in the corner of the lab. Design teachers make things that do not work, and then make them better. And so on.

'Lifelong learning', if we are willing to accept the challenge, has to mean so much more than lifelong consumption of accredited courses. Teaching for lifelong learning is quite the opposite of teaching people to become lifelong students. It is teaching them to be pioneers and explorers. And the most powerful way to do that is to be an example. When Albert Einstein was asked for his thoughts on education, he replied that he thought the only rational method of educating was to be an example. And he added ruefully, "If you can't help it, be a warning example". We know only too well what examples of bad learning are like. They are defensive and narrow-minded, full of shallow 'certainties' and afraid ever to admit ignorance or uncertainty. Their whole identity is bound up with being knowledgeable and 'right', and they hate to be wrong or feel out of control.

If education is to help all youngsters become good lifelong learners, we have to people their lives with shining examples of learning, and make sure that, when they are faced with warning examples, they see them as such, and learn what not to be.

From the Secretary of State for Education upwards, downwards and sideways, through PGCE courses and headteacher trainings, we need to making sure that everyone in education is being the role model they can be, and that young people meet adults who are genuinely resourceful, honest, and never afraid to say: "I don't know".

[1] *Industrial Society, Speaking Up, Speaking Out! The 2020 Vision Programme Report*, The Industrial Society, 1997

[2] Carol Dweck, *Self-Theories: Their Role in Motivation, Personality and Development*, Psychology Press, 1999

[3] Guy Claxton, *Wise Up: The Challenge of Lifelong Learning*, Bloomsbury, 1999

[4] John Holt, *How Children Learn*, Penguin, 1965

[5] Rachel Marcon, *'Fourth-grade slump: the cause and cure'*, Principal, May 1995

[6] Howard Gardner, *The Unschooled Mind*, Basic Books, 1991

[7] Stephen Lynn and Johanna Rhue, *'The fantasy-prone person: hypnosis, creativity and imagination'*, Journal of Personality and Social Psychology, vol 51, 1986

[8] Guy Claxton, *Hare Brain, Tortoise Mind: Why Intelligence Increases When You Think Less*, Fourth Estate, 1997

[9] Ellen Langer, *The Power of Mindful Learning*, Addison-Wesley, 1997

Learning to go with the grain of the brain

John Abbott and Terry Ryan

IF YOUNG PEOPLE ARE TO BE EQUIPPED effectively to meet the challenges of the 21st century it is surely prudent to seek out the very best understandings from current scientific research into the nature of how humans learn before considering further reform of the current system.

Let me give you an analogy. We humans have been using our brains to think as long as we have been using our stomachs to nourish our bodies. We think we understand both processes well: they are both a matter of common sense. Yet, with the breakthroughs in the understanding of diet in the last 30 years, we are eating better and now live longer. This analogy is useful when we look at the brain and the opportunities that now present themselves to expand its capabilities. We are now in a far better position to understand the brain's adaptive functions, what we know as 'learning'.

Researchers in the 1990s have uncovered a massive amount of evidence in the cognitive sciences, and in neurobiology, evolutionary biology, evolutionary psychology, and even in archaeology and anthropology, which shows us in great detail how it is that humans actually learn. We now can see why learning is much more than just the flip-side of good teaching and schooling. Much of this evidence confirms what many people have always intuitively thought; learning involves far more than schooling. People are quick to recognise that many successful public figures were either school failures or removed themselves from formal schooling early. Conversely many successful people in school seem to have disappeared without a trace.

Why? Not surprisingly, long-term studies show that the greatest predictors of success at university are:
1) the quantity and quality of the discussion in the child's home before entering school;
2) the amount of independent reading, regardless of subject matter, which the child did for him or herself.
3) the clarity of value systems as under stood and practised;
4) strong positive peer group pressure; and
5) the primary school.

Still further down the list is the secondary school. Formal schooling is only part of what fires up the inquisitiveness in a child's mind.

The human mind
Children's learning is the most natural and innate of human skills; humans are born to learn. It is what we are better at than any other species. As a result of brain imaging technologies, researchers are now able literally to watch learning occur as specific patterns of brain activity within the brain light up on a computer screen. The unprecedented clarity that this technology

reveals about brain function is causing scientists to revise many of their earlier assumptions about how individual learning actually takes place. These findings have undermined the behaviourist metaphor of the brain as a blank slate waiting for information. The brain is now seen as a far more flexible, self-adjusting, biological metaphor, the brain as a living, unique, ever-changing organism that grows and reshapes itself in response to challenge, with elements that wither through lack of use. The mass of evidence that is now emerging about learning and brain development has spawned a movement towards educational practice which confirms that thinking skills, metacognition, as well as significant aspects of intelligence, are learnable.

The prestigious Santa Fe Institute noted in 1995, in a collection of essays entitled *The Mind, the Brain and Complex Adaptive Systems,*[1] the mismatch between emerging learning theory and dominant educational practice when they wrote;

"The method people naturally employ to acquire knowledge is largely unsupported by traditional classroom practice. The human mind is better equipped to gather information about the world by operating within it than by reading about it, hearing lectures on it, or studying abstract models of it".

These new understandings about human learning and the brain question the long-term effectiveness of plans among many governments to place increasing emphasis on the role of the school and the classroom in young people's learning.

Most school reform movements have been within the existing paradigm of pupils,

teachers and schools, whereas what is now needed is that out-of-the-box thinking which starts more broadly by focusing on the brain's ability to learn and how we become ever more effective humans. Only then can we think about how to develop and nurture appropriate learning environments.

We are who-we-are in large part because of our species' evolutionary experience over millions of years. Those experiences are firmly encapsulated in all of our brains, with each of us carrying all those predispositions that previous generations found useful to their survival. The work of the Dartmouth cognitive neuroscientist, Michael Gazzaniga, shows that life is largely about discovering what is already built into our brains. He warns that,

"all the ways that human societies try to change minds and to change how humans truly interact with the environment are doomed to fail. Indeed, societies fail when they preach at their populations. They tend to succeed when they allow each individual to discover what millions of years of evolution have already bestowed upon mind and body".[2]

Evolution, we now understand, has provided humans with a powerful toolkit of predispositions that go a long way in explaining our ability to learn language, cooperate successfully in groups, think across problems, plan for the future, and how to empathise with others. Predispositions provide individuals with a whole range of skills that enable them to relate flexibly to their environment. Yet, because for most of human history Man tended to live in relatively small groups, these skills have to be developed collaboratively as very few people ever possess all these attributes. The speed with which our predispositions evolve seems to be incredibly slow, and it is thought there have been no major changes in the last 30,000 years.

By melding neurological discoveries in an evolutionary framework researchers can see how, within a single generation the influences of millions of years of evolution mingle with the priorities of a particular culture. As was stated graphically by the Harvard Business Review in late 1998 "you can take man out of the Stone Age, but you can't take the Stone Age out of man". We are enormously empowered by an array of evolved predispositions which enable us to adapt to vastly different sorts of circumstances, yet these evolved predispositions inhibit us as well.

We have to be cautious to devise learning environments that take such predispositions beyond 'what comes naturally,' but the evidence is striking: in doing this we must go with the grain of the brain.

That 'grain' we can now begin to understand far better. The relationship between nature and nurture is well summarised by the English Professor of psychobiology Henry Plotkin in his 1996 book *Evolution in Mind*, Plotkin notes that "nature has itself evolved. Nurture can only be fully understood in the light of historical causes. Nature has nurture".[3] This goes a long way towards explaining just why humans learn the way they do.

Harvard's Howard Gardner uses his theory of multiple intelligences to show that, deep within our minds, we have multiple survival strategies that include an ability to look at any situation from a number of different perspectives. Link this with the emerging understanding of how the neural structures of the brain grow, and we begin to get an understanding of how these different forms of intelligence enable each of us to make sense of our environments in very different ways. These 'different ways' are critical to our species survival, and help provide insight into the origins of creativity. The balance between emotion and logic, the role of intuition, and the relationship between intrinsic and extrinsic motivation are all part of the 'complex adaptive system' that best describes the brain's ability to deal with the messiness of ordinary everyday life situations.

The brain and effective learning

Now, consider what we know about the brain and effective learning in light of the many systems developed over the past 150 years to organise individuals within an industrial economy.   Prosperity meant organising people into factories where their broadly based skills were not needed and very quickly, in support of this, school systems were built which emphasised functional transactional skills that only utilised a small proportion of each individual brain. Such underused brains had to find their satisfaction elsewhere, and factory owners were quick to replace intrinsic motivation with extrinsic reward.

Our present 'crisis in schools' partly relates to the collapse of the old factory system and the recognition that successful workers now have to have more than just basic skills and an amenable attitude, which is largely what was required of their parents and grandparents.

Things are now very different. As the Pulitzer Prize Winning author Daniel Yergin recently observed:

"companies are being forced to think differently...that means fostering a culture that encourages alertness, responsiveness, and flexibility, and the speeding up of the cycle time of processes and decisions. In the aftermath of 'reengineering' and restructuring, competitive forces now demand a rediscovery of employees and of the knowledge they command...The high-rise pyramids of hierarchical corporate structures are being transformed into the low-rise of the flatter organisation, less bureaucracy, more teamwork, and a greater dispersion of responsibility, information and decision making". [4]

In short, we need people who are competent problem-solvers, creative, flexible and personally responsible for their welfare and the welfare of those in their family and neighbourhood.

Research from the evolutionary sciences show that these collaborative higher order skills and attitudes are indeed largely innate. Thus, with only a limited amount of stimulation at an early age (as would have been the case in pre-industrial times) they quickly develop. Despite six, eight or ten generations of such limited demands being placed on our sense-making skills, our genetic inheritance has not yet been modified a jot. Children are still born with latent predispositions, as it were, equipping them to take on the world. During much of this century formal schooling has struggled to provide appropriate simulation of real life situations. It has met, inevitably, with only limited success.

For those who have been able to succeed in abstract terms, there are as many for whom schooling has been a disaster because they are more practically orientated. Industrial

society had no place for children in the world of adult affairs. Children were seen to be in the way. So we are stuck with a system which has progressively turned childhood into an ever more extended virtual holiday. In reality we have trivialised adolescence, by denying adolescents the opportunity of learning from their own experiences, and making them good processors of information provided by other people.

However, it is only very recently that researchers have come to understand this. Such learning theory that existed in the late 19th and early 20th centuries was generally behaviourist – people needed rewards to do tasks; our brains were blank sheets awaiting instruction; and intelligence was dimly thought of as being completely innate and inherited. So, as England and its territories developed an education system for the masses (initially as much to keep children off the streets as to give them useful skills), so this rapidly came to reflect the industrial factory model.

When universities were asked to advise on the curriculum they did so by suggesting a highly reductionist model of learning. To such early educational experts the study of learning was a strictly academic affair. They measured what happened in classrooms when people performed abstract tasks, but they hardly ever deigned to study the calculating ability of an apprentice working on the job, such as Benjamin Franklin, or a street trader on the Whitechapel Road in the East End of London.

This late 19th century compromise between the scientific understandings of the day, the needs of industry, and the desire to give all children basic skills, increased productivity and lifted standards of living most significantly. But this came at a cost. Deep down many children became deeply frustrated, with so much of their latent predispositions just untapped by the daily routine of instruction. The daily challenge of making sense of their environment had been replaced by a dull recognition of waiting to be told what to do and how to do it.

Societies now stand at a very exciting time in human history, at an evolutionary crossroads. Will we be able to capitalise on these understandings and reverse what is now seen as an upside down and inside out system of education?

Everything that we understand about our intellectual development suggests that below the age of seven or eight, particularly below the age of three, we are heavily dependent on external encouragement and stimulation to develop the brain in ways in which survival skills (the ability to collaborate and see across issues) develop. If such skills are not stimulated at an early stage then learning them later on is simply far more difficult. In late twentieth century terms the functional skills of reading, writing, and numeracy also fit into the category of survival skills. At an early stage of life every youngster needs to make great demands on adults if he or she is to master these basic survival skills. While adults may be ambivalent about their roles as parents and caregivers, to a child good parenting is utterly essential if their mental faculties and social skills are to develop.

The natural tendency of young people when they move into puberty is to reverse their dependency on adults. They want to be in

control; not because they want to be bloody minded, but because all the hormonal changes going on within are pressing them to show that they can now use what they learnt earlier to become fully functional, independent people. If they are not equipped with the basic survival skills described earlier, then adolescents are desperately ill-prepared to deal with the physiological changes of adolescence and end up mentally, emotionally and socially adrift.

Changing current models

Now, consider today's model of schooling. In elementary schools in very many countries the largest classes are when children are very young; thus, when predispositions are at their most fertile, we have children in classes of 30 or more. In secondary school we have ever decreasing class sizes which clash with the adolescent's increasing wish to be independent at about the age of 14 or 15. Many adolescents, for the most natural of reasons, get completely turned off by schooling at this stage because it simply does not seem real in comparison to the emotionally charged environments they experience away from school with their peers. To remedy this upside down and inside out model of learning we have got to go back to the main line of the development of the human brain as was largely being practised before the introduction of the industrial model of schooling. Such a model of learning would be based on a set of arrangements that mirrors, as far as possible, the biological process involved in weaning. It requires the development of a pedagogy that emphasises the young child's mastery of a range of skills, and that child's embryonic but growing ability to take responsibility for directing their own work and realising that they will be doing this for a lifetime. As early as possible the system must aim to get the child to be a worker. It is no longer enough for them to simply be recipients. As children get older their learning must be integrated into the broader life of the community, with real tasks for young people to do, and real responsibilities for them to shoulder.

Elementary schools should provide classes for five year olds of no more than 10 or 12. Teachers should construct learning programs which combine, in the child's mind as well as theirs, an understanding of both content and process in ways which make children's thinking visible to themselves. This will significantly change the role of the teacher making it essential for them to model the very techniques of good learning that children will need for themselves. While good teachers will remain essential it is clear that successful learning for all will require substantially more than just the technology of teacher, chalk and talk. As a policy, investment in the technologies of learning should increase with the child's age.

Now let us briefly turn to the inside out part of the current model of learning. Young people spend no more than 20 percent of their waking hours between the ages of five and 18 in a classroom. However, within the community at large there are an ever increasing number of early retired people who are fit and strong and have many professional skills. At the moment they are largely wasted in terms of helping young people's learning. Such people may not want to become teachers, but many would be interested in sharing their expertise with young people informally. These are just the people that adolescents need to be able to relate to, almost surrogate grandparents. These people need to be recruited to work with young people.

If a formal education system starts with classes of 10 or 12, but limits overall expenditure to no more than at the present, that would suggest classes of 40 or more at the age of 18. But that need not be the case. If schools do their job properly, and children get such intensive support in the earliest years, then it would actually be better for them if, probably before the age of 16, little more than half their classes were formally taught. For much of the time it would be more helpful to them if they learnt to work on their own, and accessed the rich learning resources that schools and community mentors would then be able to provide. Too much instruction makes young people too dependent on the teacher.

We now have it within our power to construct models of learning which go with the grain of the brain, while at the same time reconnecting adults and children outside the formal setting of a school.

---

[1] Harold Morovitz, *The Mind, The Brain and Complex Adaptive Systems,* Addison-Wesley, 1995

[2] Michael Gazzanga, *The Mind's Past,* University of California Press, 1998

[3] Henry Plotkin, *Evolution in Mind,* The Penguin Press, 1997

[4] Daniel Yergin and Joseph Stanislaw, *The Commanding Heights,* Simon and Schuster, 1998

A view from the classroom

Michelle Paule

THERE IS A WORRYINGLY CONTEMPORARY passage in Jane Austen's *Mansfield Park* which indicates her concern with educational practices and attitudes to learning.[1] In this passage, the young Bertram sisters display wonder and contempt for their cousin Fanny Price's educational deficiencies, she cannot, for example, list the principal rivers in Russia, or repeat the chronological order of the kings of England. Their aunt chides the girls, telling them that not everyone is blessed with powers of memory equal to their own, and reminds them that they still have a great deal to learn. "Yes" replies Maria Bertram, "till I am seventeen".

Here we can see Austen exposing two areas of concern: that formal education focuses on a narrow range of competences, and that young people therefore regard it as a largely irrelevant process which finishes with school. *Mansfield Park* was published in 1814. At the beginning of the second millennium, why do such attitudes still prevail, and what are schools doing to address them?

The National Curriculum prescribes what children should learn and what skills they should possess. But on the range of means by which such skills and knowledge may be acquired and demonstrated this otherwise detailed document has little to say. It is not difficult to see why it has evolved in this way. Knowledge of content is easy to assess

through nationally standardised testing; prescribing content gives a sense of control, and moreover, traditional, content driven teaching and learning perhaps reflects the educational experiences of the generation responsible for its creation.

I would argue that the current curriculum model can inhibit learning through restricting the range and creativity of classroom experiences, and results in far too large a proportion of students feeling that education is chiefly a process of accumulating information, a process which they are only too happy to dispense with at the end of school.

The fact that meeting exhaustive content requirements can result in the edging out of the tools and skills needed to access the same curriculum has been recognised. The Literacy and Numeracy initiatives bear witness to this. However, such initiatives alone may still only support the acquisition of a narrow range of learning skills, contributing to making education feel like a frenetic commuter trip, rather than a voyage of discovery. What is still lacking is a cohesive and coherent approach to the development of cognitive processes themselves, and a widening of perceptions of learning.

The challenge of the curriculum
Speaking at the 1998 Potential into Performance conference at St Catherine's

College, Oxford, Professor Diane Montgomery of Middlesex University made the following points:

- That didactic methods which rely heavily on verbal exposition and questioning are found to be the least effective teaching method, even for the highly able.
- That effective learning is associated with teaching which incorporates cognitive skills and which embraces flexibility, problem solving, creativity, collaboration and offers some autonomy for learners in constructing their own knowledge.
- That such an underlying 'cognitive curriculum' is the least recognised of those (such as moral, social etc) which schools should provide alongside the National Curriculum, and tends to be learned incidentally.[2]

The DfEE itself states that

> "we want to see more examples of accelerated learning based on the latest understanding of how people learn [and of] the systematic teaching of thinking skills, which research has shown to be strongly associated with positive learning outcomes".[3]

It is not only the Government and researchers who have identified the problem. Students themselves perceive the effect of a content driven curriculum on the nature and quality of their learning experiences, as is shown by the recent MORI Attitudes to Learning survey by the Campaign for Learning.[4] Students report that lessons are "dominated by copying from the board or a book, 56% and listening to the teacher talk for a long time, 37%." Here we see they are often passive receivers of information, with the processing of such information as a largely solitary act, dependent on skills in copying,

listening and note-taking. Successful learning through such methods is moreover dependent on high-order, often subject specific literacy skills, an area in which many students felt least skilled and most anxious. Moreover, the exam system itself is based on a narrow range of competencies; it relies heavily on an understanding of prescribed content assessed through formal writing skills. Given these constraints it is understandable that most teaching is based around these approaches.

The effects of such a limited range of learning experiences, and means of testing which demand high performance skills in a narrow range of competencies, can be clearly seen in the attitudes towards learning with which many students arrive at my own school. This is an Upper School in a city three tier system, bordering housing estates characterised by the highest levels of social deprivation in the city. Levels of attainment on entry are low; this year, 27% of incoming year 9 students were achieving at the expected level in English, with the percentage in Maths and Science being only slightly higher. In practical terms, this means that the majority has difficulty accessing the curriculum at the required level. In human terms, it can mean that these students do not perceive themselves as learners, have little experience of success in learning processes, and tend to be characterised by over-dependence on their teachers, resisting taking responsibility for their own learning, and becoming anxious or uncooperative.

The relationship between experience of learning, self-perception and motivation is illustrated by Sallyanne Greenwood and Becky Green in *English and Ability* who state that:

"the rationale for raising standards through the National Curriculum, its attendant assessment methodologies and reporting procedures, seems to be based on the erroneous view that a scarcity of rewards in a competitive climate will motivate children to try harder and thus achieve more".[5]

This statement is followed by a table of ten levels, which seems immediately familiar to teachers, as it adopts the format and language of National Curriculum assessment criteria. However, these levels do not illustrate the characteristic levels of achievement, but of motivation. Hence students at the lowest levels should be able to: Conclude from accumulated evidence that ability is low and will always be; expect failure in all situations and opt out entirely; find alternative sources of success and self esteem.

As one reads up through the scale of levels, a pattern emerges of low confidence and teacher dependence. It is only at the highest levels that confidence, independence, risk-taking and personal satisfaction become identifiable characteristics of learners.

However, able students often suffer from a peer group culture, which does not value achievement. They are reluctant to appear to be high achievers, developing a range of strategies to avoid being noticed in the classroom. This can be particularly true of boys. *The Times Educational Supplement* carried a range of features on Summer Schools for the most able throughout the summer of 2000, many making the point that at such summer schools students experience a reprieve from the 'anti-boffin' attitudes which prevail in many classrooms. Such attitudes can be seen to be the inevitable result of systems of learning which reward the minority who have the ability to perform a narrow range of skills to a high order.

If a culture of achievement in which learning is given due status is to be created, then learning itself has to become something in which the majority can successfully participate. We need to change our student's perceptions of themselves as learners, through changing their learning experiences. The challenge then for teachers is to ensure the delivery of content, but to do so via a cognitive curriculum, which exposes and enriches the processes of learning.

The issue of skills

Developing thinking skills in the classroom equips students to go beyond information given, to question, explore and make judgements. Learning becomes a process of discovering meaning and pattern, and is essentially interactive. Most importantly, skills necessary for success are explicitly taught rather than assumed.

This year, I have been undertaking a Skills Audit, both in my school and with other colleagues in Oxfordshire, working with individual teachers and departments to gain an overview of the range of skills demanded across the curriculum and how these are being taught, through analysis of schemes of work. The purpose of the audit is to improve differentiation in terms of ranges of conceptual challenge rather than level or volume of content.

What the audit has revealed is that many teachers feel that their subject is more concerned with content than with skills; teachers of Science, Business Studies and Humanities are most likely to feel this, and teachers of English, Modern Foreign Languages, PE and ICT least so.

The skills most frequently identified by teachers as necessary for success are those related to literacy, such as taking notes, constructing paragraphs, writing reports and essays, and reading for information - areas already being addressed though whole school literacy initiatives. Through discussion, however, a range of underlying processes have been exposed – for example, the need to interpret, analyse, select and order information, and draw conclusions before beginning an essay in any subject. It is the consideration of these skills that is having has the greatest impact on lesson planning. Hence one can now not only find the conventions of report writing being taught in a Maths lesson, but mind-mapping and mnemonics in English; students instructing teachers in the complex narrative conventions of graphic novels in Literacy Support; and students discussing their research with confident reference to their own learning processes in Business Studies. The enthusiastic response of students where a greater range of learning strategies and intelligences are employed, and where subject specific literacy demands are specifically taught is clear. There is an evident correlation between increased confidence, motivation and higher attainment.

In general, teachers are confident discussing the content of their teaching, and in assessing the degree to which students are successful in terms of outcome with great accuracy. However, most are more cautious when considering the processes of skills acquisition. Given that learning styles and cognitive processes do not usually figure any more largely in teacher training at secondary level

than they do in the National Curriculum, this is hardly surprising. It is clearly important that initial teacher training courses begin to address this area, but how is the training of serving teachers to be managed?

Montgomery's research suggests that modest changes in general teaching methods can incorporate cognitive process strategies which can improve the learning opportunities of all learners.[6] My own skills audit supports this view. What has been most encouraging has been teacher interest in the initiative as a means of developing practice. This may be partly because while it is concerned with developing learning processes, and ultimately with increased exam success, it does not involve change to or increase in curriculum content. In a profession afflicted with initiative overload, and increasingly driven by league table anxiety, these concerns must figure large. At secondary level in particular, while acknowledging that there are a range of thinking skills which are subject specific, for example in science or mathematics, I think that such a cross-curricular model whereby learning processes are enhanced across all lessons must have more impact than separately timetabled lessons devoted to cognitive development.

Teachers as learners

Before this can have any sort of large scale implementation or impact, however, we teachers have to become learners. As Montgomery states, "If teachers are to make changes in their teaching methods then they have to be taught by those very methods."[7] Many of us have experienced poorly delivered INSET in which we are required to sit for unendurable periods of time as passive listeners while being fed the latest initiative. Whatever the merits or demerits of the training subject, we quickly become bored and demotivated, and experience a frustration over our lack of control. This is familiar territory, and there is little so guaranteed to make us identify with our students. If teacher training in cognitive development is delivered via interactive learning processes, we might expect to see the same positive results that we do in the classroom - increased motivation, heightened self-esteem and a willingness to take responsibility for our learning, take risks and face challenges.

If we are to expect our students to take with them attitudes and aptitudes which define them as lifelong learners, then learning must be for them a process which is accessible, relevant, and over which they have some control. Furthermore, we must build into our curriculum the notion that learning is a lifelong process.

One of the most interesting initiatives to have impact on students perceived as low achieving and poorly motivated is the Youth Award scheme. This is a timetabled course for 14-16 year olds, taken as an alternative to a GCSE subject. In following the course, students select and complete a range of challenges in consultation with their teacher. Once they have completed the required number, they are awarded their Bronze, Silver or Gold level.   What makes this course such a departure from their usual school experience is the degree of control they have, and the breadth of the range of challenges. They encompass, for example, skills and understanding in health, citizenship, sport, literacy and numeracy. Many tasks involve processes such as discussion, problem solving, investigating and prioritising. Challenges can also be supervised by a parent or employer, thus involving learning

experiences outside the classroom. Some challenges are undertaken alone, others in collaboration. Thus any lesson might involve one student planning and making a healthy packed lunch, another making a formal telephone enquiry, yet another researching a topic in the library or on the internet, while a further group complete a sporting challenge outside. In each case, students are aware of the purpose of the challenge, and the skills focus. The course clearly develops confidence, social skills, learning and study skills. Students are guided towards tasks which may be challenging but are accessible, and the rewarding of completed skills is immediate. The teacher remains in an active, managing role, but the students experience a range of flexibility and degree of control over their learning hitherto unknown to them.

While such a course will not be relevant for all, it is possible to extract certain features which it may be possible to extend to other curriculum areas. The range of skills involved, and the degree to which learning experiences normally occurring outside the classroom are brought inside and accredited seem to me to have great potential.

One of the greatest developments which we can exploit to extend learning possibilities at school and beyond is of course computer technology. In the classroom, computers offer not only access to information, but opportunities for both independent and interactive learning. Many schools now offer learning opportunities via intra-net systems, where students can pick up and continue work at home, e-mailing work back to school. Distance learning is an increasingly popular form of delivering training for teachers, for example, the New Opportunities Fund ICT training, and the

Excellence in Cities initiative both use CD ROMS and e-mail conferencing. Importantly, learning via the computer is not perceived by students as an activity which takes place solely at school or that is participated in solely by people of school age. My school is fortunate in having a joint community use library through which local people have access to computers, so not only is there access to the network outside school hours, but students become used to the sight of local people coming in to the library to work and learn. We also run family technology events, and loan laptops to students for home use.

These are small beginnings but betray enormous potential. If this potential is realised, I hope that schools like mine will one day be regarded as learning centres, where not only qualifications for the next stage are gained, but skills and practices are developed for a lifetime's learning.

[1] Jane Austen, *Mansfield Park*, Penguin Books, 1994

[2] Professor Diane Montgomery, speaking at St Catherine's College, Oxford University 1998 Conference, 'Potential into Performance'.

[3] DfEE, *Excellence in Schools,* DfEE, July 1997

[4] Bill Lucas and Toby Greany, *Learning to Learn: setting the agenda for schools in the 21st century,* Campaign for Learning, 2000

[5] Sallyanne Greenwood and Becky Green, *English and Ability*, David Fulton, 1994

[6] Professor Diane Montgomery, speaking at St Catherine's College, Oxford University 1998 Conference, 'Potential into Performance'.

[7] Professor Diane Montgomery, speaking at St Catherine's College, Oxford University 1998 Conference, 'Potential into Performance'.

High expectations and standards for all: the essential context for creating the Learning Age

Michael Barber

SINCE ITS ELECTION IN MAY 1997, THE Labour government has begun, with passion and purpose, to turn into a reality the commitment by Tony Blair in opposition, to make his top three priorities "education, education and education".

The Government's vision is of a world class education service, one which matches the best anywhere on the planet. We want to see this achieved, not at some indeterminate date in the future, but as soon as possible within the decade that has just begun. Our sense of urgency comes not just from the belief that every day when a child's education is less than optimal is another day lost, but also from the belief that time is running out for the public education system to prove its worth.

The reforms described in this chapter address one of the Department for Education and Employment's overarching objectives, namely to ensure that:

"all young people reach 16 with the skills attitudes and personal qualities that will give them a secure foundation for lifelong learning, work and citizenship in a rapidly changing world."[1]

We believe that successful reform of schools is possible, that they can meet the needs and aspirations of all pupils in our diverse, modern societies and that it need not take forever. That is the vision before us.

The opportunity

In England we have an opportunity, possibly unique, to achieve that vision across an entire system of twenty four thousand schools and seven million pupils. The current government has a large majority. Expenditure on education is increasing in real terms year-on-year, with over five per cent real growth last year, more than eight per cent in 2000 and three further years of real growth now agreed.

In seeking to achieve this vision we are highly conscious of our starting point. In a 1995 study of adult literacy[2] the UK fell behind most European countries and Australia, performing similarly to the United States. In maths for 13 year olds, in the 1995 TIMSS[3], England fell below the OECD average. Meanwhile the proportion leaving school unqualified or with low levels of qualification is unacceptability high compared to other developed countries. Clearly, this relatively poor starting point provides a greater impetus to reform.

In the modern world, though, electorates are fickle and impatient. They do not take the words of politicians on trust. Why should they? They may be prepared to give a new government a little time to settle in, but only a little. Much as they might share the long-term vision of a world class education service, they will not wait patiently for five or ten years to see if it is delivered. They want immediate evidence that it is on the way. Hence the central paradox facing education reformers in a democracy: a long-term strategy will only succeed if it delivers short-term results.

High-challenge, high support

In order to move from the evidently under-performing system of the mid-1990s to the world class vision and to do so while generating short-term results, we have developed a policy approach best described as 'high challenge, high support', which is illustrated below.

It is possible, by generalising ruthlessly, to see this diagram representing 25 years of educational history in England: ten years of low challenge and low support until, in the mid-1980s, the Thatcher government turned its attention to the problems of the education service. Their answer was to increase the challenge: new standards, new tests, new school inspection, new publication of school test scores. Ten years of high challenge/low support followed. The increased challenge was not matched by investment in teachers' pay, smaller classes, improved technology, professional development or better school buildings. Nor was enough done to address the social circumstances which, particularly in declining industrial areas and large cities, made the job of educators daily more difficult. The result was some improvement but also conflict and demoralisation.

During those conflicts many educators waited for the election of a Labour government

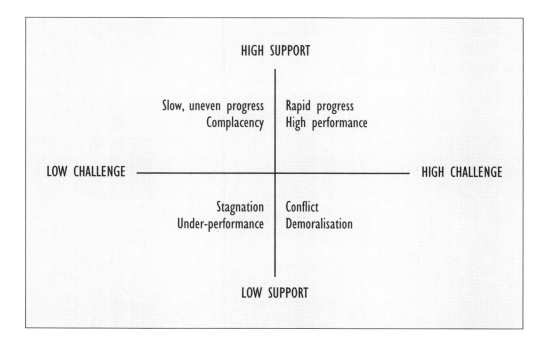

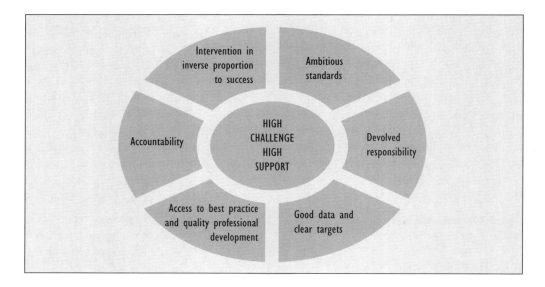

which, the historical evidence suggested, would reduce the challenge and increase the support. But the Blair government did not believe the old approach would deliver either the long-term vision or the short-term results. Instead it built on the Conservative government's reforms, sharpened the challenge and, crucially, added the support. Hence high challenge/high support.

The framework for continuous improvement

The way in which these principles of high challenge, high support are turned into practical policies which will drive school improvement is shown in the diagram above.

In order to achieve the step change we require, three broad strategies have been developed and implemented, each one aligned with and reinforcing the framework for continuous improvement. These are:
• the national literacy and numeracy strategies at primary level;
• the transformation of secondary education;
• the modernisation of the teaching profession.

The national literacy and numeracy strategies

We will never create the Learning Age unless virtually all children learn to read, write and calculate to high standards before they leave primary school. At the time of the 1997 election the national data showed how far we were from achieving this goal. Only just over half of eleven year olds were meeting the standards set for their age in literacy and numeracy.

Within a few days of that election the new government set ambitious national targets for the year 2002: that in literacy eighty per cent and numeracy seventy five per cent of eleven year-olds should meet the standards set for their age. These targets are staging posts on the way to even higher levels of performance by the middle of this decade. These kinds of standards are the essential building blocks of a society in which everyone can be a lifelong learner: we are determined not to give up on any child to deny him or her this essential right.

To achieve these ambitious objectives we have progressively put in place a comprehensive and aligned national strategy that is now well known.

The impact of the strategies so far is evident in the national test results over the last three years. Continued improvements in test scores will be crucial to the credibility of the Government reforms. It is important to remember, though, that test results are only a representation. In the case of the tests we use, they are a good representation, but what matters most is the reality of what pupils in schools know, understand and are able to do. The most heartening evidence so far of the impact of the strategy is not last year's test scores, but the fact that teachers and heads can see the difference day-to-day in the capacity of their pupils.

Our intention is to pursue the strategies consistently, to refine them constantly and to invest in professional development for primary teachers through to 2004 at least. Each year the professional development programme will be based on analysis of what pupils and teachers have (and have not) been able to do well the previous year. Precision-targeting of professional development across a system is one of our most important strategy innovations, ensuring both quality and cost-effectiveness.

While the overall strategy impacts directly on teaching, learning and pupil achievement, we also recognise that developing lifelong learners requires a much broader series of other measures designed to provide the necessary underpinning. The Government's innovations in this area include:
* pre-school education has been introduced for all four year-olds whose parents want it

and for around 60 per cent of three year-olds;
* class sizes for 5, 6 and 7 year-olds are being reduced to a maximum of 30 across the system;
* learning mentors are being provided to help remove barriers to learning outside school from thousands of primary age pupils in the disadvantaged parts of our large cities;
* after-school and/or summer learning opportunities are being offered in over 25 per cent of primary schools;
* campaigns, including government-funded television advertisements, have been run to promote parental support for reading and mathematics;
* the National Year of Reading (in 1998-9) and Maths Year 2000 have opened up opportunities for businesses, community groups, libraries, churches and others to join the national crusade;
* family literacy schemes are supporting parents whose own levels of literacy prevent them from assisting their children as much as they would like;
* growing investment, year-on-year, is being made to provide extra assistance in literacy and maths for children whose first language is not English.

The result of these measures is not only to strengthen the capacity of the system to deliver the demanding targets but also – to use the phrase of a school principal from El Paso – to take all the excuses off the table.

The transformation of secondary education

In our drive for world class performance and the creation of a culture of lifelong learning, the next phase demands that we modernise secondary education so that it builds on the growing success of the primary sector rather than, as at present, dissipating it. If pupils leave secondary schools ill-equipped and poorly motivated to learn, then creating the Learning Age will remain a mirage in a sad desert of under-achievement.

Our data shows that currently in the middle years (age 11 to 14):
• around 30 per cent of pupils have regressed in English and maths a year after leaving primary school;
• the quality of teaching is poorer than for any other age group;
• pupils make less progress than in other phases, especially in science;
• the gap in performance between girls and boys, already evident at age 11, widens significantly;
• the performance of black pupils, especially boys, slips dramatically;
• secondary schools with concentrations of pupils whose prior experience of learning has been uninspiring and whose present social circumstances are characterised by poverty, face an enormous challenge;
• there is immense variation in performance among our secondary schools, even after controlling for intake.

In these circumstances it is not surprising that many aspirant parents of all classes, especially in the large conurbations, are sceptical about publicly-provided secondary education. A key goal politically, socially and educationally is to convince this group that we can deliver a service which meets the needs and the aspirations of their children.

Our strategy for doing so has two elements:
• a universal strategy to improve the quality of teaching and learning and therefore improve achievement for all pupils aged 11 to 14;
• a targeted programme called 'Excellence in Cities' designed to promote both equity and diversity in England's major conurbations.

Teaching and learning in the middle years (age 11–14)

Our intention over the next three years is to design and implement a strategy for the middle years which will be of comparable thoroughness and quality to the national literacy and numeracy strategies at primary level but which takes account of the greater complexity of secondary schools and the secondary curriculum.   Its main characteristics will be:

• new annual targets for schools and LEAs relating to the performance of 14 year-olds and national targets for 2004;
• new tests for age 12 and 13 (in addition to those already in place for 11 and 14 year-olds) to check that all pupils are making progress and that those who had not met national standards in literacy and numeracy by age 11 are catching up;
• extending the primary school strategies for literacy and numeracy into the middle years, including materials, a professional development programme and extra assistance for schools facing the greatest challenge;
• improving transfer arrangements from primary to secondary schools including funding summer school provision aimed at transferring pupils in almost half of secondary schools;
• new teaching programmes for all curriculum subjects available electronically and traditionally from this month;
• the preparation and provision of professional development opportunities for all teachers in every subject;

• the preparation and provision of professional development opportunities in 'transforming teaching and learning' available to all secondary teachers and including the teaching of thinking skills, assessment against standards, student engagement and individual student-level target-setting.

Each aspect of this comprehensive programme will be trialled over the next two years starting in about 200 secondary schools this September. From September 2001 it will be extended and by September 2002, the full programme should be in place and making an impact on every one of our 4000 secondary schools.

Excellence in Cities (EiC)

EiC is a programme designed to transform both the reality and perception of secondary education in England's largest conurbations. Its purpose is to convince both parents and pupils that publicly-provided education can meet both their needs and aspirations. If the programme is to succeed, it will need to guarantee high standards for all in the essential core of learning and, simultaneously, open up individual pathways and aspirations for each student. In short it will need to provide both equity and diversity.

We have developed four core beliefs which inform every decision from national level to individual classroom. The statement we sent to participating schools is outlined in the box (right and on the next page).

The programme has only been operational for about a year, but already there have been substantial reductions in truancy and exclusion and improvements in pupil attitude. The programme is hugely popular with teachers and principals. It has broken down

the isolation of many inner city schools and encouraged a new sense of shared endeavour. We believe these are "vital signs" of improvement. Ultimately the programme should result in a complete re-engineering of secondary education. Instead of fitting pupils into the system as we did in the 20th century, we would build the system around the needs and aspirations of learners – a true Learning Age aspiration.

1. High expectations of every individual

EiC will encourage all schools to have high expectations of every individual pupil and all young people to have high expectations of themselves. It will seek to meet the needs and aspirations of all young people whatever their gifts and talents and to remove systematically the barriers to their learning, whether inside or outside the school. No pupil's education should be confined or restricted because of the school they happen to attend.

2. Diversity

EiC is designed to increase the diversity of provision in secondary education in the major conurbations. Diversity will differ dramatically from the past in two important respects. Firstly – as with the Government's wider approach – it is not for a few at the expense of the many. Through city learning centres, many secondary schools will take on specialist functions in addition to their core function of providing a good rounded education for all their pupils.

Secondly, the additional resources a school receives under the programme are designed to bring higher performance, not just to that school, but to other schools in the area too.

3. Networks

EiC is based firmly on the belief that schools working together, collaboratively, can achieve more for pupils, parents and communities than schools working in isolation. Of course, each individual school is responsible for continuously improving its own performance. But by working with others to share best practice, tackle common problems and offer specialist opportunities to pupils from a range of schools, each school can help to enhance performance across an area. Promoting diversity, recognising excellence and disseminating good practice are essential to these networks working effectively.

Each pupil should see him or herself as a member, not just of a specific school community, but of a wider learning community committed to his or her success.

4. Extending opportunity

Some schools in large conurbations have always succeeded. Yet others, often close by, have suffered. The EiC programme is intended to bring success to every school rather than concentrate it in a few locations. The investment that the EiC programme brings to an area should therefore extend opportunity. Rather than reinforcing current inequalities, it should enhance quality. Its purpose is to make Excellence for Everyone a reality rather than just a slogan.

To turn these beliefs into reality there are seven strands of the policy which deal with gifted and talented pupils, removing barriers to learning, behaviour support, beacon schools, specialist schools, new city learning centres and Education Action Zones.

The modernisation of the teaching profession

No matter how coherent our framework for school improvement, no matter how successful our policies to strengthen primary and secondary education, world class standards will elude us unless we can recruit, retain and develop teachers and school leaders of real quality. We face major challenges in doing so. There are major teacher shortages in some secondary subjects including science, maths, modern foreign languages and music. Schools in challenging circumstances face particular recruitment and retention difficulties. There is a shortage of good candidates for leadership positions, especially at primary levels. All of the above are particularly acute in London and the South East, where the cost of living is much higher.

Beyond the challenges of recruitment and retention are other serious problems. While, at the cutting edge of change there are growing numbers of teachers and school leaders who are embracing reform, the general culture in the profession is characterised by anxiety about change, sensitivity to criticism, and a sense of being overburdened. Also there is a pervasive belief, to some extent justified, that society does not value teachers sufficiently. The Government's reform programme, with its powerful critique of the status quo, is simultaneously the short-term cause of some of this, as well as being the long-term solution. Either way, it is evident that, as the economy continues to boom, the education service will find itself competing ever more fiercely with the rapidly growing demands of the new economy for talented graduates. It is against this background that the Government is implementing the most radical reform of the teaching profession since the second world war.

In order to address these problems – some immediate, others still emerging – before they became acute, the Government published proposals for a comprehensive reform of the teaching profession in December 1998. The programme outlined at that time, modified slightly in the light of consultation, is currently being implemented. The new vision of a modernised teaching profession has five aspects.

1. Strengthening leadership

The framework for school improvement, with its emphasis on schools themselves taking responsibility for their own destiny, puts a high premium on leadership. It may be a simplification to say that the difference between success and failure is the quality of the head teacher but it is not far from the truth. In the turnaround of failing schools, for example, a change of head has been necessary in around 75 per cent of cases. The systemic problem is clear. The people currently in or on the brink of leadership positions have been promoted with the expectation of administering the traditional education system, only to reach the top and find it in a process of radical transformation. Their careers have prepared them to manage a system which no longer exists. Instead of managing stability they have to lead change. In place of an emphasis on smooth administration, they find an unrelenting focus on pupil outcomes.

Our task as a government is to attract and develop a new generation of school leaders and to enable the present generation to adapt to this radically new and demanding world.

2. Linking pay and performance

The central challenge for us, as for many other education systems, is to recruit good people into teaching, enable those who are demonstrably successful to rise rapidly and improve the status of teachers in their own eyes and those of the public. Linking teachers' pay to their performance is the key to achieving these objectives. In addition to raising the pay of all teachers by more than inflation, we will introduce in the next twelve months:

- a new performance threshold for teachers seven years into their careers or earlier if they are exceptional: their performance will be assessed by their headteacher and an external assessor against published standards which include the impact of their work on pupil performance. All those who meet the standard will receive a £2K pay rise which will be consolidated, permanently, into their pay;
- a performance management system under which heads must assess every teacher's contribution annually in improving performance of both pupils and the school;
- two routes to higher pay above the threshold, one for taking on management and administration, the other for being an outstanding teacher; the historic complaint of teachers ("the only way to get promoted is to stop teaching") has been answered;
- a School Achievement Award Scheme which will provide lump sum bonuses to be distributed among the staff of those schools which demonstrate substantial improvement or sustained excellence; about 30 per cent of schools will benefit.

The proposals, in particular the Government's insistence that pupil outcomes must be taken into account in assessing teacher performance, have been controversial within the teaching profession but broadly supported outside it. We have developed them partly because, to anyone outside the teaching profession, it is simply not credible to leave the central purpose of an activity out of the assessment of it, and partly because our wider objective is to create a culture in the education service in which everyone, whatever their role, takes responsibility for pupil performance.

3. Improving professional development

For most teachers professional development has traditionally been haphazard, off-site, barely relevant, poorly provided and a chore at best. I exaggerate, but not much. If we are to create an education service capable of both achieving world class standards and changing rapidly, we know we have to do much better. Even more fundamentally, if we are seeking to create a Learning Age, then it is vital that teachers are themselves lifelong learners and that they model these behaviours in front of their pupils.

We are significantly increasing investment in professional development year-on-year but the issue is at least as much one of the nature and quality of provision. Across the country as a whole, expenditure on professional development is likely to exceed 5 per cent of the total teachers' salary bill for the first time, in 2001. To improve quality as well as quantity we have:

- developed the capacity to organise and deliver professional development of quality to all teachers on themes of high national priority, such as literacy and numeracy in primary schools;
- begun to put in place arrangements to ensure that each school, in addition to its mainstream devolved budget, has a clearly identified, separate pot of money for professional development designed to support its own improvement strategy;
- developed programmes, most currently in

their pilot phase, to encourage individual teachers to see their own professional development as a right and a responsibility. Among them are state-funded individual learning accounts for teachers in disadvantaged areas, research scholarships and international exchange opportunities;
- sought to enhance the capacity of teachers to provide professional development for their peers through the creation of beacon schools, advanced skills teacher posts and, for national priorities, the creation of networks of exemplary professionals such as our 2,000 leading maths teachers, each given several days a year to share good teaching practice with colleagues in other schools;
- established a General Teaching Council to promote higher professional standards and improve the status of the profession.

4. Strengthening the preparation of teachers

While our professional development reforms are improving the skills of the existing teaching force, we are also seeking to improve the training and preparation of new entrants. Our reforms to date have:

- imposed a new National Curriculum for initial teacher training setting out the standards and content of training courses which all providers must follow;
- introduced training salaries of £6K (£13K for teachers of shortage subjects) for good graduates doing post-graduate training or for mature entrants joining teaching through the employment-based routes;
- required for all newly qualified teachers an induction year with a lighter timetable and clear standards for achievement by the end of the year;
- run television and cinema advertising

promoting teaching as a career;

• developed plans for a fast-track route into teaching for exceptional candidates of any age, with extra intensive training, extra pay and extra responsibility.

These measures are designed to lead into the wider reforms, allowing talented teachers to progress more rapidly than ever. It is too early to say what their impact will be, but applications for initial teacher training are up significantly since the new training salaries were announced.

5. Providing greater support

Teaching is demanding work at any time. During a period of rapid change and high public profile it is exceptionally demanding. If teachers are to be successful in the future, we will need to enable them to prioritise teaching, learning and their own professional development and simultaneously to relieve them of the other demands on their time. So far we have not achieved the balance we would want, but a number of measures are beginning to make a difference:

• a major investment in school buildings, staff facilities and ICT;

• the provision of standards, teaching materials, planning guidance, data and best practice advice through the internet (the Standards Site had 17,000 pages searched on Christmas Day 1999!);

• making provision for, and encouraging, the use of technical expertise to maintain ICT systems, manage school budgets etc;

• training and developing over 20,000 additional classroom aides, particularly to support literacy and numeracy teaching in primary schools;

• reducing bureaucratic burdens on schools and teachers by streamlining administrative systems.

The problems

By any standards the Government's reform programme is an ambitious one and I believe it will work and achieve our objective of creating a world class system. No-one, however, is likely to believe my account or share my optimism unless I draw attention to the problems and "messiness" which accompany this reform, just as they accompany any major programme of change. Indeed, as I write this, it would not be no exaggeration for me to say it is at a critical stage.

A great many elements are currently in intensive implementation – literacy, numeracy, the pay threshold, performance management and training for ICT, for example. The capacity of the system (not to mention many individual headteachers and teachers), is stretched to the limit. Only if each element of the reform is well-planned and implemented can we achieve successful and irreversible reform.

Our success in bringing about irreversible reform will depend on our ability to address deep-seated problems, and minimise their negative consequences, while sustaining the implementation of the overall strategy until all pupils achieve high standards, no matter what.

Towards a Learning Age

The present phase of reform is all-embracing and urgent but, even as it is implemented, it is important to look ahead and to anticipate the shape of reform to come. I want to finish this chapter with some speculations about the future.

The first task is to see things through. It may seem a statement of the obvious, but the first task in the next three to five years is to embed the reforms currently being put in place and ensure they become irreversible.

The literacy and numeracy strategies at primary level need to be constantly refined and built upon for at least another four years so that every primary teacher's skills reach high levels. The performance management system needs to ensure that every teacher is focused on the quality of their teaching so that all students achieve high standards. The system needs to develop the capacity to prevent failure and tackle it after it has occurred.

All this is not about new reforms but ensuring the present ones work. The last twenty years of education reform are littered with programmes which have been inadequately implemented or abandoned by governments without the courage or strategic sense to see them through to impact on student performance. We will not make that mistake.

If it all works, the result will be schools with high autonomy and performance. The policy principle of intervention in inverse proportion to success is being applied steadily. If our overall strategy works, as more schools succeed, so they will have greater autonomy and reward. Ultimately each school would have substantial autonomy. Each would have responsibility for meeting standards in the core areas of learning, but also making a distinctive contribution to the system as a whole. The autonomy would not be unconditional. It would have been earned, because performance had been demonstrated. Government's role in these circumstances would shift from driving reform to creating the conditions and, crucially, the culture for a transformation which would be led and created by the schools themselves.

School reform will globalise. Just as financial services globalised in the 1980s and media and communications in the 1990s, so in this decade we will see education reform globalising. The impact of the international comparisons of the 1990s, such as TIMSS,[4] was profound. Increasingly researchers and policy-makers have extended their horizons beyond national boundaries in the search for solutions.

This process will go much further as technological change and globalisation gather pace. The death of distance, best characterised by e-business, will not leave schools untouched. We will see the globalisation of large elements of the curriculum. We, in England, will want to be sure that our 14 year olds are as well educated as pupils in the USA, Germany or Singapore, not least because ultimately they will be competing in a global job market. In any case, physics is the same in Kentucky as it is in Kent. Media and communications organisations will prepare and market internationally excellent interactive materials which will influence curriculum, standards, pedagogy and assessment across international boundaries. They will also re-engineer where and how learning takes place. It is hard to predict how this will happen: successful school systems will be those open-minded and sensitive enough to spot it when it does.

The school will remain crucial to providing the foundation of learning, the induction into democratic society and the constant support that every individual student needs, but it will cease to be the provider of all learning for each student. Instead, while it will provide some, it will also seek learning opportunities in other schools, in out-of-school learning settings (such as museums), in the community, in the workplace or over the internet. It will be an advocate for the student and a guarantor of quality. Increasingly teachers and heads will think not just outside the boundaries of their school building, but beyond their city and their country too.

This process will truly represent the opening up of schools to the wider lifelong learning system that the 21st century will witness. To anticipate this in England we intend to provide international exchange opportunities for 5,000 teachers a year and from next year, through the new Leadership College, offer every head the opportunity to link to his or her peers abroad.

The central question for public authorities will cease to be "who provides?" Instead they will ask "how is the public interest to be secured?" We must ask ourselves from where the energy, knowledge, imagination, skill and investment will come to meet the immense challenge of education reform over the next decade.

For most of the 20th century, the drive for educational progress came from the public sector, often in combination with the religious or voluntary sectors. Towards the end of 20th century, as frustration with existing systems grew, this legacy was challenged by a growing vibrant private sector, especially in the USA, but also in many other parts of the world, including China, Africa and South America. The challenge for the 21st century is surely to seek out what works. The issue is not whether the public, private or voluntary sector alone will shape the future but what partnerships and combinations of the three will make the most difference to student performance.

There is a rich field for research and development here and we need to know more. The central challenge is to build social coalitions in the drive for higher standards and radical reform. It is clear in Hong Kong and elsewhere that the business and religious sectors are strong allies. This is true in the USA. It is clear in Eastern Europe, where the Soros Foundation is investing heavily in early years education. Each a different combination but each fit for their purpose.

Public authorities will need to invest more in education than ever before, partly because of technology and pressures to improve teachers' pay, conditions and professional development but mainly because they will be striving to achieve much higher performance standards for all, not just some, pupils. Meanwhile, those parents who are able to will spend more money than ever on their children's education. Some may choose private schools, depending on the quality of public provision locally, but many will spend on resources for the home and on out-of-school learning opportunities of all kinds.

The challenge for government will therefore be to provide not only high quality schools, but also the equivalent of the home and out-of-school learning opportunities for those students whose parents do not have the will or the means to provide them. This will be crucial from an equity as well as a performance point of view and opens up an entirely new area for public policy.

---

[1] DfEE Objective 1, *Learning and working together for the future*, DfEE, 1998

[2] J. S. Carey, S.Low and J.Hansbro, *Adult Literacy in Britain:* summary of key findings for the Office of National Statistics, London, 1996

[3] The Third International Mathematics and Science Study, Washington D.C., 1995

[4] The Third International Mathematics and Science Study, Washington D.C., 1995

Inclusive learning

Martin Stephenson

EDUCATION IS THE UNIVERSAL SERVICE FOR children and young people and, because of this, it is arguably the central dynamic of social inclusion. Compulsory education involves 15,000 hours of a child's life and schools are anchors of local communities. Consequently probably the greatest single risk factor in a person commencing a long-term 'career' of social exclusion is becoming detached from mainstream education and training.[1] A young person who cannot gain access to mainstream education, or who has significant difficulties participating there, is effectively not a full member of the local community, and is less likely to become an active citizen or participate in lifelong learning.

If we frame social exclusion in this way, we locate responsibility with our institutions and professional cultures, and at the same time recognise the diverse needs of young people. Current professional and political opinions often tend to focus on the difficulties and 'disaffection' of the children and young people, rather than on the duty of public services to meet the needs of all children and young people.

The scale of disconnection

Best estimates indicate that approximately 350,000 13–19 year-olds are, at any point in time, detached from mainstream education and training or employment.[2] These young people are not a discrete, homogenous group, although they are likely to share disadvantages relating to their physical and

mental health, their housing and family stability.[3] These factors have a complex interrelationship with a young person's participation and progression in education, which, in turn, creates further risk factors.

While we must recognise the complexity of the problems that socially excluded young people face, we should not consider their needs entirely separately from those of the majority. Nor should we aim to construct a simple continuum of need, from a high academic achiever free from problems through to a young person permanently excluded from school and rebounding between the care and criminal justice systems. There is enormous variation in children and young people's responses to the multiple adversities they may experience. There are also large numbers of young people, not obviously socially excluded, but signally underachieving and failing to participate effectively at school. Equally there are high academic achievers who are insufficiently challenged or need guidance in coping with critical events in their lives.

The diagram on the next page illustrates the flows of young people out of mainstream secondary schools and into other services. It does, however, give a misleading impression of an ordered system: the reality is that interactions between the education, social care, health and criminal justice systems are often chaotic. This results from the sheer complexity of inter-organisational relationships, the speed at which events happen, the

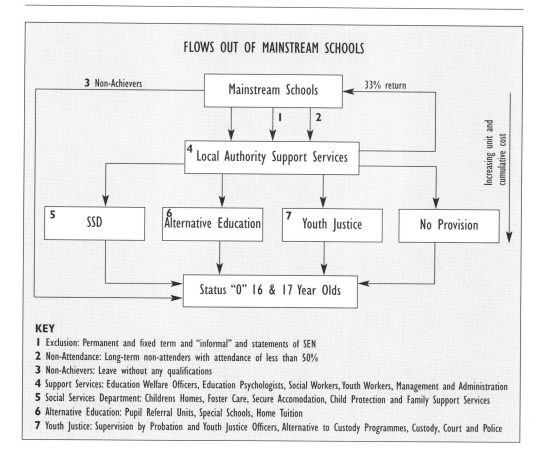

FLOWS OUT OF MAINSTREAM SCHOOLS

KEY
1 Exclusion: Permanent and fixed term and "informal" and statements of SEN
2 Non-Attendance: Long-term non-attenders with attendance of less than 50%
3 Non-Achievers: Leave without any qualifications
4 Support Services: Education Welfare Officers, Education Psychologists, Social Workers, Youth Workers, Management and Administration
5 Social Services Department: Childrens Homes, Foster Care, Secure Accomodation, Child Protection and Family Support Services
6 Alternative Education: Pupil Referral Units, Special Schools, Home Tuition
7 Youth Justice: Supervision by Probation and Youth Justice Officers, Alternative to Custody Programmes, Custody, Court and Police

lack of one single accountable professional, and the agencies' very different legislative, funding and cultural backgrounds.[4] The cumulative effect of such interactions is often to ratchet a young person further away from mainstream education and life with the majority of their peers.

The failure of segregation

It has to be accepted that conceptually and practically, exclusion has its attractions. Formal permanent exclusion from school is set in the context of a public disciplinary process and at school level usually appears as a rational, if last-resort, solution to an in-tractable problem. However, at a macro level it is extremely counterproductive: it has negative impacts on the young person's life, participation in learning and likely association with criminality, as well as the budgets of other agencies.[5]

Exclusion is symptomatic of two approaches that are features of our legal and social welfare systems: 'segregate to punish' and 'segregate to nurture'. In practice these have overlapped for nearly 150 years in the UK, fuelling the growth in the nineteenth century of residential institutions for juvenile offenders and children separated from families or deemed uneducable.[6] Today, excluded pupils still tend to be segregated in off-site units, known as Pupil Referral Units since the 1993 Education Act.

But the enforced segregation model has fundamental flaws. Research into juvenile criminality suggests that becoming part of delinquent peer groups is a significant risk factor for offending.[7] So a model that places young people together on the basis of their anti-social behaviour and encourages them to form a group, in a very different environment from mainstream school, would appear to have a limited chance of success in terms of equipping them for a return to mainstream school. Even positive behaviour, when it is learned in 'abnormal' environments, will not easily survive the challenge of transferring to a school, college or workplace.[8]

Research and inspections have revealed serious weaknesses in segregated provision:
• the curriculum tends to be narrow;
• the quality of teaching can be reduced by the lack of specialist subject teachers;
• there is often a wide range of ages in a single unit, which can mean inappropriate role models for younger pupils and a long-term, out-of-school culture that hinders their reintegration; and
• academic achievement and progression into further education, training and employment are often unacceptably low.[9]

It therefore looks unlikely that the problem of exclusion can be resolved simply by increasing resources to PRUs, particularly given the requirement that LEAs must provide full-time high-quality education to all permanently excluded young people by 2002. Even assuming that the annual rate of exclusion falls by the one-third required in the Government's target (that is, to 8,200 by 2002) there would still need to be a virtual doubling of national provision.

A new response

The challenge is to design a programme of social inclusion that is truly universal and brings about a step-change in access, effective participation and progression for all children and young people.

It would be relatively easy to focus on the arguments for inclusion as a model for social justice, but a workable system must also take full account of the day-to-day realities faced by practitioners who balance the competing demands of SATs, Ofsted inspections and performance appraisal with potential changes to their pedagogy. But fundamental change is clearly necessary, and the concepts of exclusion and inclusion offer real opportunities and practical benefits to all who engage with learners.[10]

Inclusion is a comprehensive, continuous process of ensuring young people's access to, effective participation and progression within mainstream education. It demands a system that can:

• recognise and reduce exclusionary pressures on young people and professionals;
• create support systems and resources that enable all young people to navigate transitions, surmount barriers to learning and cope with critical life events; and
• enable our institutions and professions to evolve, adapt and become resilient in themselves.

If we are to embed this within our professional cultures, policies and practices, our education system faces two major challenges.

The first problem is the concept of 'universal'. In policy formulation, 'universal' is too often just code for 'the majority' or 'the norm'. In a diverse, multi-cultural society, the design and implementation of truly universal education services presents a real challenge for policy makers and practitioners. The departure point cannot simply be 'the norm', or a 'deficit model' that starts from the needs of the excluded. We need to distinguish inclusion from the deficit model of reintegration – a serious blockage in the current system. Around two thirds of pupils excluded from secondary school do not return; and no research has evaluated the progression of those that do.[11] Inclusion goes beyond access to a new school for a permanently excluded young person; that is just the starting point. Nor can inclusion mean assimilation: it must acknowledge racial, cultural and religious diversity.[12] And while inclusive practice is essential for young people experiencing particular barriers to learning, it should not become only a synonym for special education.

The second challenge is to embed the concept of universal inclusion in mainstream education as a priority for all, to be discharged through schools and other public services. If inclusive practice is understood simply to mean returning young people with challenging behaviour to school, it will understandably be perceived negatively, by teachers as an added pressure, and by headteachers as an intrusion on their authority. Other agencies may also express resistance in the context of their own operational priorities; removing barriers to learning inevitably involves social care, housing, criminal justice and health issues.

Inclusive practice must encompass the needs of all learners, and be sensitive to the changing role of the school and the functions and relationships of teachers and other practitioners.

Inclusive practice

It is possible to draw a parallel between the dominant mode of production in an economy and the shape of its public institutions and services. The design of our schools and children's homes, and our approaches to teaching and learning have been influenced as they developed by the pervasive metaphor of the factory. We can see our public services still as characterised by concentrations of capital and labour, rigidly demarcated functions and hierarchical systems.[13] But services now play a greater role in our economy than manufacturing; globalisation and the e-economy are changing how we communicate and do business. Our teaching and learning systems need a corresponding flexibility, with an emphasis not on production but connection.

A universal, inclusive education service must enable learners to connect and stay connected. Each person needs the skills to manage their own learning; to plot a course through diverse environments, experiences, institutions and jobs; to manage information in many aspects of life; and to exercise informed individual choice. This need underscores the importance of equipping people for lifelong learning, but it also shows the potential for social exclusion to become further entrenched. To reduce the risk of this, we need to help learners develop their resilience and acquire the critical new planning skills.

Resilience is the ability to cope with threats, uncertainties and critical life events. It is a concept relevant to all children and young people given the pace of change in most dimensions of life, but particularly those at risk of social exclusion. Although the evidence is sparse at this stage, resilience appears to be a significant protective factor against disconnection from learning. Schools can have an important influence on the development of resilience; and studies have found that schools make an impact on young people's ability to plan their lives. Where this impact is positive, young people from high-risk backgrounds are less likely to join peer groups with anti-social behaviour, which has a beneficial impact on their life choices.[14]

Alongside resilience, we need to foster individual planning skills. Progression in learning and employment increasingly depends on individuals' ability to set objectives, detail the steps necessary to achieve them, establish priority tasks and review progress. It can be extremely demanding to manage transitions and make choices in environments of rapid change. It is all the more demanding for a young person with multiple problems, that perhaps include health and social care deficits that have restricted the development of their basic skills and self-esteem.

A truly universal approach would be for every young person to be entitled to an Individual Learning Plan as the Campaign for Learning suggested in 1996. This would be the hub of all assessment work relating to needs that affected their access, participation and progression in learning. All professionals, in social care, criminal justice, health and specialist areas of education, would undertake their assessment and planning work under the umbrella of the Individual Learning Plan. The minimum requirements would be that their planning was complementary, that there was uniformity of practice and standardisation of the instruments used.[15]

An inclusive system, focused on enabling young learners to make and maintain their own connections to learning, needs to be built through three key areas:
- a connective curriculum;
- a connective pedagogy;
- connective professionals.

A connective curriculum

A broad and interlinked concept of career guidance needs to underpin inclusive practice, with personal, health and social education (PHSE) seen as integral in helping pupils to prepare for the range of roles they will experience in life. PHSE now increasingly links careers education with, for example, sex education, financial capability and citizenship.

But in addition to changes to the substance of the curriculum, changes in the way it is delivered can also help to facilitate inclusive learning. ICT represents an enormous opportunity to connect young people firmly to learning. Teenagers are the fastest-growing group of online users: 60 per cent are now online, compared with 44 percent in 1999. Ninety five per cent of homes have a fixed phone line and an increasing number of young people use a mobile phone.

Through ICT, the entire concept of mainstream education can be expanded to include diverse learning situations. It can enable young people who move home or care placement to keep in touch with their original school; it can facilitate transition and reintegration to a new school. Smart card technology can help to manage incentive schemes for teenage learners on a national scale, making new linkages across different learning activities and institutions. However, there is a clear correlation between levels of household income and ownership of PCs; those individuals in most need of connection to learning may lose out. With only tenuous ties to mainstream education, a young person has fewer opportunities to acquire the skills to access ICT.[16]

The school has a critical role as a web of connections and in putting inclusion at the heart of its culture, policies and practice. We cannot afford for inclusion to be viewed as yet another 'initiative' to which schools and teachers must respond. It is critical to ensure that the potential of inclusive practice to remove barriers to learning and therefore increase educational progression is widely understood; and aligned and integrated with existing school development planning processes.[17]

Connective pedagogy

The concept of inclusion poses pedagogic challenges, particularly when there is such an emphasis on improving standards, often through relatively prescriptive approaches such as the National Literacy Strategy. An inclusive approach does not accept that a different kind of teaching is necessary for students who are socially excluded, rather the extension and refinement of widely applicable methods of teaching.

The concept of a connective pedagogy has recently been proposed; one which "combines the importance of teaching which relates to individual learners while connecting individuals within their social context".[18] A key assumption underlies this approach: all students possess the ability to acquire new skills and patterns of behaviour can be modified. It follows that mainstream education is the appropriate context for this teaching. A connective pedagogy suggests that if education attempts to meet the needs of the minority in

isolation from the majority, it could constrain the learning of both. A teacher has to connect with individuals as well as connecting them within the school and with the wider community. The needs of the minority and majority should be connected through a differentiated curriculum and appropriate pedagogy; that is, a range of teaching methods and styles designed to meet common, specific and individual educational needs.

Connective professionals

Profound changes are occurring in the way in which consumers are accessing goods and services. As the business sector responds to globalisation and e-commerce, the delivery of public services is also being shaped by ICT and the internet, from NHS Direct to e-counselling. These developments have the potential to transform the professional landscape; indeed the concepts of professions and professional practice as we know them may ultimately be challenged.

At the same time the recognition has grown that for young people, social exclusion can often result directly from the lack of a coherent, co-ordinated service architecture. The division of responsibilities and functions between local authority departments, schools and health authorities creates faultlines, which are compounded by different professional cultures. They result in multiple professional interventions, and a diffusion of accountability for outcomes. The Social Exclusion Unit has emphasised that a key barrier to securing inclusion in the current structure is the fact that "no single institution is responsible for ensuring that young people find a suitable option or even necessarily knows what has become of them".[19]

To address this structural fragmentation and its exclusionary pressures, we need a new profession – a learning broker. Above all this means a single point of contact for the young person: one professional who can assess risk factors in an integrated way, offer individual support, broker services where necessary to enable the young person to thrive in the mainstream, and assist in their reintegration if they have been excluded from it.

The need for accountability to rest with a single individual has grown at the same time as a range of 'intermediary' services; personal brokering, coaching or advisory services. As consumers are offered rapid access to a potentially bewildering array of goods and services, the role of professionals or specialists as dispensers of first-line information decreases and people have more need of brokers, coaches or guides – in public services as well as in the commercial sector.

It is no coincidence that policy reforms in a wide range of settings have advocated new roles incorporating elements of brokerage or guidance: Learning Mentors in secondary schools, Young Person's Advisers for care leavers and New Deal Advisers within the Employment Service.

We are witnessing the emergence of a new sector of activity, which coheres around some core skills. The new Connexions service has the potential to bring about a step-change in inclusion within schools, representing an attempt to bring much-needed coherence to a whole range of services both internal and external to the school: aiming for synergy rather than substitution.

In tandem with a rapid expansion of call centre and internet services that offer 24 hour, seven days a week brokerage, information, advice and guidance to young people, Personal Advisers will work with both individuals and groups to enable them to develop their autonomy as learners, their willingness and capacity to plan, and their coping strategies. They will contribute to the development of an inclusive school and ensure that in turn it is connected to the wider community.[20]

These Personal Advisers will also focus on reconnecting young people to learning by addressing the range of problems that they may be facing and brokering additional specialist support where necessary. As currently envisaged, they should in time become the pre-eminent agent of connection between young people and secondary education, aiming to link them securely to learning for life. This role is clearly applicable also to primary and higher education, and has the potential to become a mainstay of lifelong learning for people of all ages and communities.

Conclusion

Lifelong learning and inclusion depend upon each other. This symbiosis can be nurtured by schools through a culture that promotes a connective curriculum and a connective pedagogy, equipping young people to navigate through the web of challenges they face in the transition to independence. Our public services, too, need to develop a more flexible, web-like response to young people's needs. We need to complete the move away from a mind-set that requires solutions based on segregated institutions and working practices for those who do not conform; and focus instead on adapting our institutions and working practices to meet all young people's needs. Inclusive learning is about removing barriers and creating flexible access to learning for everyone: the challenge for the future is how to connect.

[1] Martin Stephenson, *Reintegration to school and social inclusion*, IPPR, Autumn 2000

[2] *Education and Labour Market Status of Young People Aged 16–18 in England:1992–1998*, DfEE,1999

[3] *National Strategy for Neighbourhood Renewal, Report of Policy Action Team 12: Young People*, Social Exclusion Unit, 2000

[4] *Bridging The Gap: New Opportunities for 16–18 year olds not in Education, Employment or Training.*, Social Exclusion Unit,1999 and Adnenne Jones, and Keith Bilton, *Shape Up or Shake Up? The future of Services for Children in Need*, National Children's Bureau. 1993

[5] Carl Parsons, *Education, Exclusion and Citizenship*,1999 and Tom Bentley, Ravi Gurumurthy, *Destination Unknown*, Demos, 1999

[6] Roy Parker, *Away from home: a short history of provision for separated children*, Barnados, 1990

[7] Michael Rutter, Henri Giller and Ann Hagell, *Antisocial Behaviour By Young People*, Cambridge University Press, 1998

[8] Peter Mortimore and Chris Watkins, Pedagogy: What do we know? in *Understanding Pedagogy*, ed. Peter Mortimore, 1999

[9] Eric Blyth. and Judith Milner, Exclusions from School in *Exclusion from school: interpersonal issues for policy and practice*, eds Eric Blyth and Judith Milner, Routledge, 1996

[10] Mel Ainscow and Anthony Booth, *An Index of Social Inclusion*, 2000

[11] Carl Parsons and Keith Howlett, *Investigating the reintegration of permanently excluded young people in England*, 2000

[12] Robin Richardson and Angela Wood, *Inclusive schools, inclusive society*, 1999.

[13] David Hargreaves, 'Education', in *Life after Politics: new thinking for the 21st Century*, ed. Geoff Mulgan/ Demos, Fontana, 1997

[14] Michael Rutter, Henri Giller and Ann Hagell, *Antisocial Behaviour By Young People*, Cambridge University Press, 1998
Peter Fonagy, Miriam Steele, Howard Steele, Anna Higgitt and Mary Target, *The Theory and Practice of Resilience*, Journal of Child Psychology and Psychiatry, Vol. 35, no.2, 1994

[15] *National Strategy for Neighbourhood Renewal, Report of Policy Action Team 12: Young People*, Social Exclusion Unit, 2000 and *Connexions: The best start in life for every young person*, DfEE, 2000

[16] Don Passey, *ICT and Social inclusion*, College Research FEDA, vol.3 no.2., 2000

[17] Mary Ainscow and Anthony Booth, *An Index of Social Inclusion*, 2000

[18] Jenny Corbett and Brahm Norwich, *Learners with Special Educational Needs*, in *Understanding Pedagogy*, ed. PeterMortimore, 1999

[19] *National Strategy for Neighbourhood Renewal, Report of Policy Action Team 12: Young People*, Social Exclusion Unit, 2000

[20] DfEE, *Education and Labour Market Status of Young People Aged 16–18 in England:1992–1998*, DfEE, 1999

Out-of-school-hours learning

Kay Andrews and Mike Walton

OUT-OF-SCHOOL LEARNING IS ONE OF THE most dynamic elements of educational development across the UK today. It exemplifies a conceptual change in our understanding of where, when and how people learn. As such it opens a vital doorway between learning in school and life-wide as well as lifelong learning.

Ten years, even five years ago, out-of-hours learning activities would have been seen as completely peripheral to the 'real' business of schools. While there were still some schools which had at that time continued to make provision for pupils in a variety of ways during extra-curricular time, the shadow of the relatively new National Curriculum together with all the systems of testing and target-setting, had almost obliterated the virtues and benefits of learning outside the 'classroom'. A great many schools were deterred from setting up or supporting any such programmes, because their time was fully occupied with planning, reviewing, and re-organising.

Thankfully the picture has changed quite radically since then. A new vocabulary and new scope, new enabling frameworks, new proof of benefit, and new funding have together transformed the place and prospects of extra-curricular activities across the UK. So relevant is this work now perceived to be that it has even been given the somewhat limited official description of 'Study Support'. It has achieved sufficient status to attract funding from National Lottery grants, from the Department for Education and Employment, and from the Government via the relatively recently created New Opportunities Fund. Study Support is defined in the enabling policy document: *Extending Opportunity: A Framework for Study Support*[1] as:

> *"learning activity outside normal lessons which young people take part in voluntarily. Study Support is, accordingly, an inclusive term embracing many activities with many names and many guises".*

Significantly, the scope of Study Support is now seen to embrace not only curriculum extension activities, such as homework, study clubs or revision schemes, but enrichment activities which enable students to follow their own interests and skills, from cycle maintenance to ceramics, as well as enabling activities which bring more opportunities for personal and social skills development, community activities and voluntary work. Equally important for its links with lifelong learning has been the explicit emphasis which the new Framework and new funding has put on out-of-school learning as an opportunity for all the potential learning partners such

The online learning revolution in schools and beyond

Stephen Heppell

UNEXPECTEDLY, IT IS A VERY SPECIAL TIME FOR learning and new technologies have played a significant role in creating the fertile conditions for learning which we now find in our family, entertainment, work and education lives. When the NOP asked children for their descriptions of Internet users they did not, as their parents might have expected, suggest 'nerd' or 'geek' or 'sad' as adjectives; in fact 66% chose 'clever', whilst (friendly) (46%) and 'cool' outside (31%) made up the top three choices.[1] We have to go back in time a very long way (the Mechanics' Institutes?) to find a time when terms like clever, friendly and cool were bedfellows in youth culture.

Indeed, for most of the last century 'clever' was a very long way from fashionable. At the same time we now find that process rather than product is at the heart of our entertainment lives; at the time of writing the plasticine animation Chicken Run by Aardman Animation and Dreamworks is eagerly anticipated at the cinema. But anticipation today is not about the glitz of showbiz personality and the minutiae of detail about Nick Park, or Mel Gibson's lives, it is rather about the detail of the process that brought the film to life. By the time children and parents get to see the movie they will already have been pre-briefed, as a direct result of their hunger to unpack processes, in the details of the animators' techniques, limitations and triumphs. This is new and entirely welcome.

Even as recently as the first Oscar winning Wallace and Grommit features from the same team, we were not shown, indeed did not demand to see, process details as a necessary precursor to consumption. Often the TV programme about 'The making of' appeared a year or so later as a vague attempt to keep alive a marketing push. Listening to children leaving the cinema we find them animatedly discussing the film they have just enjoyed, not through swapping emotions ("I was so scared when the dinosaur attacked...") but through discussing technique and process ("I thought starting with that battle worked really well..."). And, of course, the immediate impact of computer technology is that for many (but not for all) these are not simply idle conjectures. They are the wise critiques of children who have the tools at home to have a go at stop frame animation with their own lumps of plasticine or at editing and tightening their own digital movies.

New opportunities of learning

At the same time the world of work has changed rapidly. Careers are short term and teams assemble in an almost organic way to engage in tasks. The workplace of the 1950s was characterised by an input output model, with vastness producing economies of scale, a product focus, factory inspectors, and quality control. The community, for many workers, was the company. In this century we find the workplace characterised by downsizing, as economies of scale can be achieved by communication technologies other than road and rail, we find an emphasis on process, with value placed on the 'C's: creativity, community, collaboration, communication, all underpinned by a strategy for quality assurance. The result of this has been that corporate Britain has stepped away from a sterile training culture to embrace a learning culture, where the learning organisation has become an aspirational objective for many companies. And work has become, once again, intellectually stimulating.

All this adds up to the unexpectedly special time for learning mentioned above: clever and friendly are cool, the tools that were formerly the unique preserve of 'experts' are increasingly available to learners everywhere, a curiosity for process is fed daily without difficulty and our job market values creativity and collaboration. What could possibly go wrong?

What will not go wrong, of course, are the expectations and aspirations of learners everywhere. Let us be clear that, although it is new technology that has given us the opportunity for so much of the change explored above, that same technology has not changed the fundamental model of learning. We learn through doing something, usually with others, always with mediation from a teacher, parent, coach or similar. We are motivated by an ipsative referencing of our own progress: we feel ourselves moving forward as learners and this is motivating; we depend on a sense of audience; we need to be inspired by passion, delight, eccentricity even; we find risk in learning exhilarating (remember when your teacher said to you in a conspiratorial way "I shouldn't tell you this yet, but I will...")? In on-line learning

communities all over the country learners are finding that what they are doing, as active learners, offers them new autonomies, new opportunities.

The power of ICT

At Ultralab the world's largest Internet learning project, Tesco Schoolnet, 2000 saw children all across the UK interviewing the oldest living person they knew for their earliest memories. Children writing in the style of favourite authors or suggesting new inventions for the future, seized their autonomy with both hands and produced a host of material by children for children. We confirmed the need for mediation from their teachers and from the project's professional facilitation team. We saw just how motivating a worldwide audience of millions could be and we enjoyed watching how children rose to the ambitious challenges of the project. In all our many on-line learning projects, with computers, with WAP phones, with wireless technology, with electronic toys even, we continually confirm just how well children of different ages work together as the young chase the role models of the older, who in turn reinforce their own understanding and self esteem by introducing new ideas to the young.

The Internet here serves as a conduit for contribution and communication (this is Information and Communication Technology, ICT, remember?) but not as a one-way delivery channel for knowledge. The children's relationship to their on-line tools is one of symmetry: they put in their own contributions just as they draw out the contributions of others. This is not an age related characteristic. Our pilot for the DfEE's virtual college of school leaders 'Talking Heads' shows how powerfully engaging and motivating the establishment of a community of practice on-line can be and how quickly the internal expertise of a community on-line can become an essential professional resource. Headteachers have poured into Talking Heads in a way that confounded cynics, those who saw head-teachers as systemic barriers to the progress of ICT in schools. As one of the adult participants in an earlier Ultralab project commented:

"The one thing that will remain with me stronger than ever, after this project is over, however, is that my fellow colleagues have perhaps a stronger sense of identity and togetherness than any other group that I have ever worked with. Yet the ironic thing is, that they hardly ever meet up, never work in the same office. And between us all, we can more or less address or find some way round any problem that any of us find...and more than that, are happy to help each other".

On-line learning works. Interestingly our research shows that the asynchronous nature of on-line learning, when the tools are right, allows a better equality and quality of contribution and greater parity of esteem between contributors than face to face, which is not to deny the need for, and pleasure of, direct social interaction. The power of asynchronous learning is confirmed by children's embracing of SMS messaging on their mobile phones; the lucky children we have equipped with WAP mobile phones confirm that this ability to slip time and thus remain in control is central to the autonomy they seek in both their learning and social lives.

Research throws up many unexpected and valuable insights. Unexpectedly, children with wireless computers in conventional class settings seem to be treated differently to children using computers connected physically to the school intranet. 'Wireless' children are seen as having a greater personal capability, resulting in teachers offering them more ambitious and stretching tasks, which the children respond to with delight, engagement and achievement. Research confirms the value of the community as a learning resource that had been too often unavailable from within the school. It confirms that, for many, the new opportunities for success and creativity that ICT offer are newly motivating and re-engage learners who were perilously near to being, or actually were, lost to the system. Common sense confirms that we ignore these newly fertile conditions for learning and the newly seductive learning environments offered by ICT at our peril.

The challenge for the school system

So, what could possibly go wrong? Sadly of course, what can go wrong are the shackles that we impose on our learners through the structures and organisation of their learning institutions and the examination system, combined with a confusion about the role and purpose of new technologies in the classroom and a mistaken belief that standards mean standardisation. Bizarrely, just as on-line learning confirms the power of mixed age learning communities we are, if anything, increasing the rigidity of our age phasing within schools. It is very, very difficult to find any reason other than administrative convenience for the grouping of large numbers of children born between adjacent Septembers.

We standardise for convenience and the curse of standardisation, of course, is that it weighs down on creativity like a damp blanket

– smothering and extinguishing. We see this at its worst after the 11 plus divide. Children (but not all children) arrive at secondary school with a vast multiplicity of delightful and creative technology experiences and capabilities: concrete poetry, plasticine stop-frame animation, digital art, science data logging, maths though Logo, web-sites, spreadsheet based explorations of complex data sets and so much more. This rich diversity changes yearly as emerging technologies allow newer, exhilarating learning experiences which (some, but not all) inspired teachers seize. Sadly many of these children, arriving in the secondary school computer lab bursting with excitement at the opportunity to show, and progress, their new skills, rush straight into the buffers of imposed uniformity.

The excited hand they wave in the air as they point out "Miss, I've got my own web site" is too often met with "I'm sure you have Dipti, but not everyone here is as lucky as you and we need to be sure that we are all starting from the same place so we will just work through this Cut and Paste exercise to make sure that we are" and another learning light is extinguished, probably for ever. The answer will never be to standardise incoming pupils' capabilities and experiences from the primary sector; the rich diversity and creativity that we see at 11 is of considerable economic value: technology offers so many diverse opportunities for learners and we are only at the beginning of learning technologies which will rapidly expand to properly embrace phones, TVs, toys even. As one of our project children reflected with a wisdom and patience beyond his years:

"My most boring lesson was in the new maths room with our teacher Miss X. She was trying to teach us the basics of Logo and there wasn't one person in the room who didn't know more than the basics already. It got pretty boring by about halfway through".

Clearly we need flexible criteria to allow us to record and value these multiplicities of appropriate progress, but we also need to value and offer continuity to higher level outcomes – for example the ability to critique sources, or make judgements about appropriate tools in different contexts – rather than focusing on simple ICT competency skills. Remember that the diversity of these competencies will increase rapidly, certainly beyond our ability to codify them.

Another barrier that frustrates the newly wired learner is schools' attitude to the legitimacy of collaboration. In on-line learning collaboration is king; the opportunity to work with new communities and to thus enrich the learning experience is listed as a prime motivator, and a key at accelerating progress, by research projects all round the world. There is a clear consensus. Collaboration is valuable economically too and in the emergent corporate learning organisation, with its focus on the four 'C's, any employee who insisted on working alone without the support and collaboration of friends would be rapidly removed from employment. Back in schools however, children caught collaborating in the examination room are ejected with the same alacrity and it is difficult to see how the one world is preparing learners for the other. It is important to remember that we are in a global race, with learning increasingly seen to be the engine that drives economies forward; on the other side of the world in Tasmania, for example, collaboration is a substantial and valued component of the compulsory curriculum because they value the social and economic outcomes that this produces.

Those examinations, and tests, are the greatest cause for concern because it is in the area of entitlement that the juggernaut of children's ambition is seen to be hurtling towards the buffers of conventional testing. There has been exceptional progress in schools to build a foundation in the skills of numeracy and literacy that are, surely, an entitlement for all learners. But many learners, often the least expected, are additionally demonstrating exceptional capability through their harnessing of ICT. "His work with the computer was a revelation" must be amongst the most common phrases exchanged in staff rooms and at parents' evenings. This successful harnessing of the computer and the engagement that results have been particularly powerful, especially for those most disadvantaged within the existing system. However, these newly motivated young learners have no sooner harnessed and demonstrated their incipient creative capabilities than it becomes apparent that the examinations and tests through

which both they and the school are judged bar computers from all examination rooms. For these learners the entitlement to evidence a capability and to demonstrate effective learning is effectively barred too. Inevitably, the lights go out on another learner as a consequence. The debate here, above all else, is about inclusion, entitlement and waste, but it is also an issue of common sense. What on earth are we doing teaching children all the sophisticated strategies of authoring with a word processor if we are to deny them an opportunity to demonstrate that capability?

Finally, it is important to reflect that the technology platform that underpins our learning, working, democratic and social lives is in a state of constant change and evolution. Policies that stand still are effectively running backwards because the expectations of learners, as they confidently harness that technology, move forward rapidly too. At Ultralab the work of Stan Owers includes

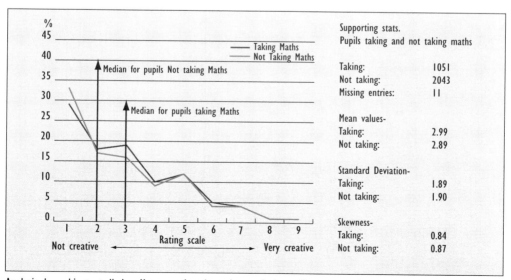

Analysis by subject studied - How creative does the curriculum allow you to be in Maths? Comparison between pupils taking Maths with pupils not taking Maths.

exploring over 3,000 A level students' attitudes to different components of the curriculum. Asked about their view of mathematics as a creative curriculum area it is not surprising that non mathematics specialists agreed that it was not creative. What is really surprising however is that the A level maths specialists agreed exactly with this view – the two graphs are close to identical.

This is new. What has changed here is not the mathematics curriculum (indeed that is the problem) but the expectations of a generation of wired school students for whom creativity, community, collaboration and communication matter enormously and are as actively sought in their learning lives as elsewhere. Ten years ago this all mattered rather less to our learners and that, above all else, is the imperative for educational change facing this country. In ten more years their patience will be exhausted and the foundations for a lifetime of learning that a fortunate combination of circumstances, together with much hard work, have offered us will have been wasted.

[1] NOP, *Kidsnet survey,* 1999/2000

Creativity, community and a new approach to schooling

Tom Bentley

FOR THE LAST HUNDRED YEARS, EDUCATION reform in the UK has followed a clear and predictable path. Since the Balfour Act of 1902, which first instituted a national system of schooling in England and Wales, the major thrust of reform has been to extend and refine the reach and impact of a particular kind of institution - the school or college. This chapter argues that, despite the pace and scale of policy change over the last ten years, we are on the threshold of a deeper and further-reaching period of transition. Government policies show partial recognition of the depth of this change, but are not yet producing a coherent, radical or long term approach to the challenges of educational innovation and restructuring.

The two most important changes to the context for education policy are: first, a transformation in the status and role of knowledge in society, leading to a very different set of demands and challenges for individual learners; second, a related change in the structure and operation of organisations across society, which poses a major challenge to the basic constitution of schools and colleges.

The challenge is best summed up in the idea that individuals must become effective lifelong learners in order to thrive. This matters not just for our economic prospects in future labour markets, but also our roles as

parents and citizens, and our capacity to achieve fulfilment and personal autonomy. However, lifelong learning, as it applies to individuals, is not enough to explain or inform the necessary transformations in the infrastructure of learning. The idea of the skilled, flexible, individual learner, adept at identifying and accessing those learning opportunities needed to keep up with the pace of external change, does not tell us enough about the social and institutional contexts which underpin learning. To achieve a learning society, we must also transform these contexts.

Two concepts are integral to understanding and achieving the kind of education system which enables 21st century societies to thrive: creativity, and community. Creativity matters because possessing knowledge in the information age is not enough, for individuals or for organisations: only those who are able to apply it in new and valued ways will be able to respond effectively to the demands and opportunities of the era. Community is central for a different reason. Learning is an activity embedded in social relationships and values. To be meaningful, it must fit a surrounding context of norms and standards. The recently developed national infrastructure for testing and inspection presents standards as an objective, technocratic domain. But learning, in the broadest sense, is evaluated according to concepts and standards which are rooted in the

structures of society. Communities therefore matter for two reasons: first, they
provide a wider context from which learners can draw guidance, motivation and
meaning for what they are trying to learn.
Second, the communities surrounding
schools and colleges can provide resources
for learning which are frequently untapped,
for reasons which I will explore below.

Institutions out of place

Twentieth century education reform is a
story of institutions. From the Balfour Act
of 1902 to the 1944 Butler Act and the
expansion of school, college and university
places in the 1960s, 1970s, and 1980s, the
underlying thrust has been to broaden participation in the formal education system,
and to increase the time spent in it by
younger generations. The current government's policies to increase nursery and early
years places, and to encourage participation
beyond age 18, are the culmination of this
trend. At the turn of the last century you
could start school at seven and finish again
at 12 or 14: extended participation was for
a narrow elite. At the turn of the twenty
first century, you can enter the public education system at three, and stay in it until 23.

This story is one of enormous social
progress, and is mirrored in many other
countries. Too often, however, it escapes
our notice that the basic form and structure
of the institutions has hardly changed.
Schools retain dominant organisational
characteristics which heavily influence the
character and quality of learning within
them. These characteristics are increasingly
at odds with the organisations and environments which learners will encounter in the
world beyond. Schools, almost without
exception, are:

- hierarchical;
- operate standardised routines and draw
  on standardised measures of performance;
- information sparse (they ration and control
  the flow of information and knowledge to
  learners);
- designed to transmit knowledge from
  expert to learner, with limited scope for
  collaboration between the two;
- subject to centralised control;
- custodial; and
- vertically integrated (that is, they organise
  teaching and administration around a
  vertical division of departments and subjects).

In contrast, they seek to prepare students to
thrive in an environment which is increasingly:
- complex;
- unpredictable;
- network-based;
- changing rapidly, with innovation and
  adaptation becoming essential skills;
- horizontally integrated (that is, projects
  and team-based collaboration are becoming
  central forms of organisation, partnerships
  and alliances between organisations are
  becoming essential);
- open;
- information rich; and
- out of control.

Public policies in creative tension

This contrast helps to illuminate current
approaches to education reform. One broad
swathe of policies, initiated during the 1980s
and continued by the current UK government, aims to improve the performance and
productivity of the existing institutional
infrastructure. In the short term, it is
working to raise conventional standards of
attainment by improving motivation, attendance, teacher effectiveness, and exam
results. Under this heading we could include

the Numeracy and Literacy strategies for primary schools, the capital works programme to rebuild and repair school fabric, league tables, the Ofsted regime, the Fresh Start programme and performance-linked pay for teachers. All of these initiatives work the existing institutions harder, seeking to produce better outputs from the same basic set of resources and structures.

A second, intertwined cluster of policies seem to aim at a different kind of target – although improving the attainment of current students is their primary short term objective, they also impact on the structure of educational institutions, and the channels through which content, instruction and guidance are accessed. These might include Excellence in Cities, in its attempt to build new urban learning networks, the National Grid for Learning, the new Leadership College, and the National Framework for Study Support. These initiatives experiment with new technologies and with network forms of organisation, and seek to draw on a wider range of resources to support learning, from on-line content to out-of-school time and community volunteers. Education Action Zones, as an explicit attempt to stimulate and learn from innovation, might also fall in this cluster, although their outcomes are still uncertain.

These latter policies are more in tune with the Government's approach to lifelong learning in the adult world. Here, through the Ufi (or *LearnDirect*), Individual Learning Accounts, and attempts to increase employer support for learning, we see a different implicit model of provision: learning activity is individualised and flexible, and takes place in a wide range of contexts. Financial investment is shared, and attempts

to change learners' behaviour are based on persuasion and incentive rather than on compulsion and direction.

The vision which supports these moves: of a society of motivated, responsible and productive adult learners, is compelling. But it is clear that the policies so far are modest, incomplete steps towards such a scenario. While the concept of lifelong learning has become familiar in policy circles, it has yet to penetrate the vocabulary or aspirations of most people. In many areas of provision the change is rhetorical, and has not radically changed the forms or patterns of educational provision.

That said, however, we are beginning to see unprecedented levels of innovation in learning, across every sphere of society. Organisations in every sector are busy inventing new ways of organising learning. There are two or three basic reasons for this. One is cultural - the more 'educated' a society becomes, the greater the demand for learning. Basic education leads to a thirst for knowledge which sustains itself over time. The second is economic - as knowledge and skills become more important as commodities, demand for qualifications rises, fuelling innovation and expansion in their provision. The third is technological. The development of a new communications infrastructure enables new ways of developing and delivering learning services. This partly means on-line access to course content, other relevant information, and guidance or assessment services. More important, in the long run, it means new ways of co-ordinating learning activity. The new technologies mean that learners can collaborate or compete through networks which are geographically unrestricted. They enable 'real-time' learning - forms of problem solving and collaboration which are embedded in the challenges and routines of other activities, rather than being conducted at one remove (within education institutions) and then applied later on to 'real-life' situations.

These changes will mean an ongoing increase in the levels of innovation associated with education. Perhaps most important, they also imply that this innovation will take place far beyond the bounds of the formal education sector. Inventing new ways to organise and evaluate learning has become an imperative for any organisation which wants to thrive. Learning is a test of its success.

A glance at the 'vanguard' sectors of the economy helps to substantiate this claim. Businesses which depend most heavily on 'pure' knowledge work - communications and media companies, for example, and management consultancies, are investing more and more in forms of learning which increase the creative potential of their employees. Even the traditional manufacturing sector is increasingly dependent on team-based learning and systematic innovation to improve the quality of products and the efficiency of production, an emphasis which places new demands on employees to contribute to the innovative capacity of the whole enterprise. The service industries, likewise, increasingly demand that employees continuously develop personal qualities and interpersonal skills which make them more responsive to customer demand and preference. The growth of corporate 'universities' is evidence of the growing need for such companies to draw on their own learning infrastructures. For all such organisations, strategies to increase and improve innovation mean strategies to develop and

refine various forms of learning. In a whole series of fields, the most successful knowledge workers are developing and modelling their own forms of learning behaviour.

Reuniting schooling and lifelong learning

What does this mean for education policy? The basic challenge seems clear. Schooling should be the foundation of an ongoing lifelong learning career, the first episode in a much longer series of encounters with learning. This role is in striking contrast with that of a century ago, when for most of the population school was the only encounter one could expect with formal education.

The great danger, however, is that the new forms of learning organisation, as they evolve in the private, voluntary and community sectors, will have little to do with the form or nature of core public education services. As a result, learners will have to rely on resources and support structures other than those provided through the school system to adapt to the environments which they encounter elsewhere.

The conventional response to changing demands on schools is to adjust the priorities and content of the curriculum. For example, as numeracy and literacy took higher priority during the late 1990s, their prominence in the primary curriculum increased. Similarly, as new 'key skills' such as communication and problem-solving were identified as important, they were added (with little success) to curriculum requirements for most courses in secondary and vocational education. Our instinctive reaction is to attempt a specification of the knowledge needed which can be incorporated into the formal expectation of what school students will learn. Schools and teachers can then be organised, pressured and incentivised to provide the outcomes specified by our collective priorities.

But this response misses the underlying thrust of the analysis. While curriculum content is important, it is only one dimension of the way in which learning is organised, assessed and modelled by education institutions. Two other dimensions are crucially important, even though they are often taken for granted in the education debate.

The first is the set of attributes, disciplines and virtues which a successful learner should develop and display. Schooling, with its emphasis on obedience, punctuality, attendance to routine, linear progress and identifying 'correct' answers, encourages a set of attributes which are less and less applicable to the challenges of our external environment. Of course, there is much that good schools can do to develop underlying positive attributes and attitudes to learning: we should not throw the baby out with the bathwater. But it is clear that schools, as institutions, remain fixed in routines and behaviours from which most other sectors are moving away.

Second, and perhaps even more influential, is the impact of the school's basic organisational structure and ethos on its ability to innovate radically in the provision of learning opportunities and experiences. The argument here is that basic aspects of the school's institutional identity - the fact, for example that all activity is governed by a centralised timetable which no longer corresponds with the routines or rhythms of any other major organisation, or the division of learning activities into a vertically separated curriculum which places formidable

barriers in the way of effective cross-disciplinary learning - will hold back the school's capacity to access and make use of new opportunities and resources for learning.

This matters for two reasons. The first is that the scope for continuous improvement in output and productivity within the existing infrastructure is limited. In the long run, it is not possible to maintain the momentum for improvement simply through incremental innovation and modest increases in public spending. The demand for education services, and for a growing range of outcomes for schools, will continue to increase faster than the capacity of government to finance it through taxation, for the reasons set out above. Moreover, if the institutional characteristics of the education infrastructure remain out of kilter with change in the wider society, it will be increasingly difficult to maintain it at current levels of performance. The current crisis in teacher recruitment is perhaps the most glaring illustration of this problem.

The second reason is that current forms of organisation impose an opportunity cost on schools. The resources potentially available to support education extend far beyond the categories we are used to debating, which usually revolve around sums of public money and the contracted skills of educational professionals. They include the financial and organisational resources of other sectors, knowledge and information which exists beyond the world of formal education, social, cultural and human resources which reside in the communities surrounding schools. New technologies, in particular, open up the channels of communication and co-ordination which could tap such resources for the benefit of learners and teachers. But to do so, we must look for ways to experiment more radically with the organisational characteristics of schooling.

Learning for a creative age

This analysis opens up a challenging agenda for educational practitioners and policymakers. But a simple increase in innovation for its own sake would produce chaos. A sustained transformation of the education system needs a guiding purpose. I have suggested that this goal should be creativity, at the individual, organisational and societal level.

This requires a shift in our definition of creativity: rather than equating it with particular groups of people, such as artists, or with natural talent or intuitive qualities, creativity should be defined as a set of capacities which can be learned. As such, creativity has as much to do with what people do not know as with what they do. It requires the ability to solve problems progressively over time, and apply previous knowledge to new situations. Creativity is also bound up with context - it can only be defined and assessed in relation to the situation in which it is achieved. It must be developed through the interaction of the learner, her underlying goals and motivations, and the resources and context in which she operates.

Our definition is relatively simple: creativity is the application of knowledge and skills in new ways to achieve a valued goal.

Four main characteristics define the creative, or progressive problem-solver:

• The ability to formulate new problems, rather than depending on others to define them;

• The ability to transfer what one learns across different contexts;
• The ability to recognise that learning is incremental involving making mistakes; and
• The capacity to focus one's attention in pursuit of a goal.

These characteristics, it is worth noting, are not specific to any particular social or age groups, or to a particular kind of organisation or institution. They are generic. As such, they can help to form a foundation for a lifelong learning agenda which cuts across our existing institutional and conceptual boundaries.

Creative learning environments

But creativity does not take place in a vacuum. Because it is not an innate personal characteristic, it cannot be understood without reference to the context in which it takes place. Context plays a significant role in determining whether one makes use of existing skills and knowledge and seeks out creative ways to build on what you already know.

Case studies and other evidence point to a number of factors which help to make an organisational environment creative:

Trust: secure, trusting relationships are essential to environments in which people are prepared to take risks and are able to learn from failure.

Freedom of action: creative application of knowledge is only possible where people are able to make real choices over what they do and how they try to do it.

Variation of context: learners need experience applying their skills in a range of contexts in order to make connections between them.

The right balance between skills and challenge: creativity emerges in environments where people are engaged in challenging activities and have the right level of skill to meet them.

Interactive exchange of knowledge and ideas: creativity is fostered in environments where ideas, feedback and evaluation are constantly exchanged, and where learners can draw on diverse sources of information and expertise.

Real world outcomes: creative ability and motivation are reinforced by the experience of making an impact such as achieving concrete outcomes or changing the way things are done.

Again, these factors are generic - they can be found in schools, companies or families. It is worth noting, though, how many of the dominant institutional characteristics of the school system seem to run against our list. A system based on routine-based learning, within a heavily standardised context, using individualised, abstract forms of assessment, and removing much of the choice from the hands of the student, does not seem well suited to developing creative potential.

Strategies for change

Elegant diagnoses are all very well. Could this kind of agenda be a basis for sustained, radical change? Schools, after all, are among the most resilient of all institutions. Accelerated reform has only been achieved by the current government at the cost of further centralisation of control. This shift, in the long run, diminishes the capacity of the whole system to innovate and generate new practical solutions. To understand and enhance the possibility of change, we have to adopt a particular view of how knowledge is created at the level of practice. My view is that radical change is possible through a combination of bold structural changes at the national level, a shift in the political climate to encourage judicious risk-taking among innovative practitioners, and a shift towards more systematic innovation at the level of school and local community.

Such a strategy is very different from either the policy blueprint model, in which change is mapped out and imposed by central decision-makers, and the traditional 'local autonomy' model, beloved of many in the education sector, in which professional integrity is interpreted as a prohibition on intervention, and a thousand flowers are left to bloom.

Three priorities stand out. The first is to reduce curriculum content. We must recognise that the scope, not just for innovation, but also for depth of understanding, is inhibited by the crowding of the National Curriculum. Rigour and depth of understanding become more, not less important for learners in a knowledge based society. If such depth is to be accompanied by increased breadth of application, then the 'coverage' of many different topics and programmes of study within curriculum subjects becomes an enemy of true understanding. Reducing National Curriculum content by half, over a period of ten years, as part of a rolling programme of curriculum development and experimentation, is therefore a reasonable, if controversial, goal.

The second is to increase opportunities for learning beyond the classroom. Between birth and the age of sixteen the average child spends only 20 per cent of her waking hours in school. Connecting what happens in school to opportunities for learning outside is therefore vital for creating a new foundation for a system of lifelong learning. New technologies play an important part here. Even more important, however, is the development of learning opportunities in other contexts: museums, workplaces, public spaces, community organisations and families. Some of this infrastructure already exists, or is being developed. Pioneering examples, such as the University of the First Age in the UK or Citizens' Schools in Boston, are showing how new forms of provision can be developed in concert with existing school routines. Excellence in Cities provides an important opportunity, in this context, to develop new learning networks. These new forms of learning activity are an important generator of social capital, and the networks in question are as much social, or human, as they are physical or electronic.

The third priority is to transform the nature of teaching. An ambitious programme to restructure and re-energise the teaching profession is already under way in England and Wales. In the long term, however, it is not enough. The impact of on-line technologies on teachers will be profound, because they undermine their historical role as the sole gatekeeper of knowledge. Teachers will retain a central role in the coordination and assessment of learning, but their ability to control and channel the flow of information to students will be dramatically undermined. The analysis also suggests that the range of people directly involved in teaching and learning will increase dramatically, to include specialist contributors, providers of learning placements, mentors, community learning co-ordinators and so on. Current government plans to develop a new category of teaching assistant are only the first step in this respect. The implications of such change are manifold, but one in particular stands out: teachers will need to model the kinds of learning behaviour which they are seeking to develop among students, and be able to apply their professional knowledge in contexts other than the classroom. It seems obvious that staying in touch with the changing worlds of work and organisation in other sectors are a precondition for such modelling, and teacher sabbaticals are already encouraged by policy. A longer term, and more radical possibility, is that the practice of teaching in schools should become part-time, and be linked to a learning specialism in another field of organisation or enquiry. Such a structural shift might also provide part of the solution to current recruitment and retention problems.

These three basic changes, though they go far beyond the scope of current policy, would provide the stimulus for far reaching change. They could all be licensed and encouraged by central policymakers, but to bear fruit they would depend on innovation at the local level. A host of other changes are also necessary, from new models of interdisciplinary teaching and learning to new forms of assessment and evaluation and new systems for managing and monitoring student attendance in a more individualised, multi-site model of schooling. New standards and safety measures for involving employers and community partners in the provision of learning opportunities would also be needed.

Schools as community centres for lifelong learning

Bob Fryer

FOR MORE THAN THIRTY YEARS NOW, EVER since Tony Crosland's famous circular on the comprehensivisation of Britain's secondary education under the Labour Government of 1966-70, schools and schooling have been almost continuously at the centre of political debate and controversy in the United Kingdom. Argument has raged over matters of pedagogy and teaching methods, the proper content of the curriculum, the issue of pupils' qualifications and results and the highly charged questions of the organisation, funding and accountability of schools. There have also repeatedly been disputes over teachers' terms and conditions of employment, the performances of schools which have been unfavourably compared with those of other countries and the contribution of schools to the country's economic competitiveness has been severely criticised.

The consequences of all of this for those most centrally involved with our schools and most directly affected by this succession of attacks, the pupils, teachers and parents, have been much the same. Scarcely knowing which way to turn next, they have been obliged to endure a climate of seemingly unending scrutiny, review, criticism, reform, reorganisation and restructuring. One could scarcely think of a better example in public life of the applicability of the simple but powerful maxim that plants will never thrive if they are constantly pulled up to see how the roots are doing. Professional morale amongst teachers has often suffered and many have sought to leave early the profession they entered with commitment, devotion and a love of teaching itself. And parents have frequently felt alienated from what is going on in the name of education and bewildered by processes that they no longer recognise from their own days at school. As for the pupils themselves, their opinions have rarely been sought and even less often been acted upon.

Schooling and society

Yet, perhaps all of this is inevitable, given the potent impact that schooling now has on our lives, both as individuals and as a country. As the last century witnessed the gradual and partial erosion of some of the most traditional, and outrageous, forms of class difference and inequality in our country, education (particularly schooling) eventually assumed a central role in the determination of the life chances of most adults. In the period after the second world war especially, the type and level of school attended and the qualifications, or lack of them, acquired in childhood and early adulthood had direct consequences for the rest of people's material, social and cultural lives.

In the second half of the twentieth century education, and schooling in particular, became the most influential factor in locating adults in the social structure of Britain. It was through their successes in school, and later in further and higher education, that many adults secured 'upward' social mobility, leaving behind the cultures and often the deprivations of childhood and home. For that minority who enjoyed the fruits of educational achievement it meant better jobs, higher incomes, more comfortable houses and improved health. Some also found the shift rather uncomfortable, the cause of unwelcome awkwardness and embarrassment amongst their family and former friends. Others sought an element of social cachet in declaiming the 'humbleness' of their working class origins. Yet others regretted the genuine losses that increasing social and geographic mobility meant in an allegedly new 'meritocratic' age.

Of course, this was not the experience of all. Only a minority of the population's children had access to the gilded privileges of private education and almost guaranteed access to university and a secure material life in the higher echelons of the professions, industry, city of London, civil service or governance of our country. For them, schooling and education beyond school simply acted as a channel and confirmation of both their advantages and cultural superiority. Schooling and education did not so much reward this minority with its manifold social privileges: it simply underlined them.

Schooling and inequality

For those outside of this cosseted minority, it is true that a share in the country's improved general educational provision and achievement at school also increasingly promised a route into our finely nuanced hierarchy of adult material wellbeing and

cultural differentiation. For those who benefited in this way from early success at school, these improvements were most welcome and, not infrequently, were fiercely defended and justified as being nothing other than the deserved consequences of sheer dedication and hard work. There was even a theory, of so-called 'deferred gratification' to explain and legitimate such hard-won prizes. Not surprisingly, parents were themselves willing to undergo all sorts of immediate personal privations and to engage in some remarkable manoeuvrings over housing and the petty politics of the school to secure success for their offspring. And who could blame them? Increasingly, as parents themselves understood, or were the beneficiaries of, success at school, they sought to deploy their domestic 'cultural capital' in the interests of their children's achievements at school.

All of this was quite understandable, if regrettable in some of its consequences for family and personal life and the inexorable pressures brought on by this striving for a modest foothold on the daunting pyramid of successful life after school. But, truth to tell, such definite advantages as were admittedly gained in this fashion were almost as nothing compared to the dogged persistence of gross inequalities of opportunity, outcome and existence in our country.

For the great majority, even with the successive impacts upon wider participation in educational achievement of the 'eleven-plus' examination and the later expansion of further and higher education, the story has continued to be quite different. Their experiences of education, and of schooling in particular, were and still are frequently either of only modest success or, far too often, of failure and of severe limitations on their aspirations and expectations. Too often their experiences and memories of school have been of boredom, irrelevance, fear, failure, humiliation, bullying and damage. Once the magic release of the minimum school-leaving age was attained, they wanted nothing more of education than, henceforth, it should simply leave them alone. Even those who were persuaded to 'stay on' into further education, as some traditional work routes for teenagers disappeared in the 1980s and 1990s and post-school opportunities expanded, did not expect to continue their education beyond the minimum necessary to secure them entry to the job-market or carry them beyond financial dependence upon their parents.

But, not even this limited, if welcome, extension of learning beyond school for the majority and the remarkably rapid expansion of participation in higher education, up to more than a third of all young people, has been enough to combat the continued obstinacy of hugely unacceptable inequalities in this country. With greater social awareness and a sensitivity forged by campaigns and self-advocacy on their own behalf by the disadvantaged, we have increasingly understood those inequalities to include unacceptable differences of gender, race, ethnicity, religion and physical disability. At a time when participation rates in higher education by young adults has already reached one third, the social class differences in those rates remain huge and unacceptable. Whilst four out of five of all young people from professional backgrounds now go on to University, only one in six from unskilled backgrounds do so. And, despite the growth in admission to higher education of mature students from a range of backgrounds,

schools and academic achievement at school are still the principal determinant of adults' chances of obtaining a degree or professional qualification.

So, the continuing paradox is that education, and schools in particular, simultaneously constitute some of the main institutional supports of inequality and hierarchy in our society at the same time as being the principal means for individuals of combating the worst effects of poor or disadvantaged beginnings. Thus schools are implicated in inequality as sites of its existence, as mechanisms for its expression and reinforcement and as routes to its continuation. Hardly surprising then that schools and schooling are identified as battlegrounds for the playing out of rival theories, practices and reforms.

Schooling, skills and civilised adulthood

The problems of the reproduction of inequalities have not been the only issues still demanding change. Schools are, of course, critically important gateways to the whole of adult life. Early achievements, and the interpretations and labels attached to young people as a consequence of their activities and attainments at school, impact upon their opportunities for developing skills and gaining access to other routes for skills acquisition. What happens to a child at school is often crucial not so much these days for the particular job or occupation taken up in later life but, more importantly, for the kind of job and the level of autonomy, choice, authority, power and material comfort that will follow in adulthood. Although this may only occur after further educational, occupational or professional qualification, attainment at school exerts a massive influence on the shape of children's later lives.

Of course, schooling has major effects, too, upon children's values and orientations, upon their sense of self and aspirations and upon their susceptibilities, including those for cultural and aesthetic expression and enjoyment. In this sense, schools are key, and often fateful, transit routes to the kinds of adults we become or are stimulated to become. Schools are also central to the public establishment and reinforcement of standards of acceptable behaviour and what it means to be a member of society or to act according to civilised values or with a sense of citizenship.

At a national level, there is also the quite proper concern with the country's overall economic performance and the role that education and training can play in improving this, building on solid foundations of early schooling. In addition to looking to schools to impart basic and contemporary key skills to all of our children, business and politicians alike have increasingly demanded that schooling prepare young people appropriately for the world of work, in terms of attitudes, competencies and expectations.

Schools and public policy

Thus, within childhood and adolescence, schooling is also one of the main institutional arenas in which public policy can attempt to make a difference, or be expected so to do. Public policy may, for example, be crafted with the explicit intention of opening up opportunities or of broadening experience and attitudes beyond those which are drawn from family life, play, interaction with peers, consumption, entertainment and so on. It is small wonder, then, that politicians of all persuasions look upon schools with an inevitably greedy and controlling eye, wanting them to be the pattern makers

and foundations for the kind of society and the sorts of adult social relations favoured by those politicians' own ideologies and priorities.

Quite rightly, this is difficult, dangerous and controversial ground. Claims and counter-claims can be expected of so-called 'political interference' or of alleged 'social engineering'. One side will accuse the other of pursuing policies that simply 'favour elites' in order to uphold privilege and maintain inequality. The other will blame its opponents' schools policy for a lowering of standards and a 'dumbing down' of achievement and the recognition of talent in the interests of securing a 'phoney' equality. In any case, we will rightly be reminded, schools cannot and should not be expected to compensate for all of the ills of the wider society.

In these circumstances, and in the context of decades of seeming constant change and turbulence for teachers, pupils and parents, it may appear particularly perverse to draw attention to the strategic importance of schools for the development of lifelong learning. With some fairness it might be contended that schools and teachers already have enough to worry about with their own immediate concerns and responsibilities, without taking on the additional burdens of lifelong learning. Moreover, it might be argued, are not the real challenges of lifelong learning to get individuals and employers to shoulder their fair share of the responsibilities and costs of learning throughout life? Surely, it will be said, the future of lifelong learning cannot all be expected to be shaped, once and for all so to speak, in the early years when schools admittedly have some influence. That is an outmoded and quite wrong conception of the relationship of education to life and utterly at odds with modern notions of continuous learning beyond school.

It will be enough, will say those of this persuasion, for schools to accomplish fully what they are really there to do, that is to ensure that all children acquire the core and basic skills for a firm foundation to be laid. The more children achieve at school, the easier will be the task of continuing learning in later life. Finally, why should yet another potentially divisive and burdensome imposition be heaped on young citizens, forcing them to become lifelong learners or else take the risk of suffering guilt and other exclusions for choosing not to accept such an uninviting summons?

The meanings and implications of lifelong learning

The force and merit of these, and related arguments, cannot entirely be denied. Indeed, if all that would be achieved by linking schools more closely to lifelong learning were the imposition of additional duties and responsibilities, more work and more risk of failure and criticism, then the undertaking would not only be undesirable, it would almost certainly also fail in its own terms. But, lifelong learning cannot be simply more of the same, other than being somehow 'spread out' more across different social groups and age cohorts. It is not just a matter of getting greater numbers involved, or of securing increased volume of provision or even of multiplying and diversifying the locales in which learning occurs, important though all of these changes are as part of the process of achieving lifelong learning.

Lifelong learning cannot be, and is not, just another 'add on' to conventional education in schools or in any other setting, bolted on but affecting no fundamental change to the original undertaking. Lifelong learning, and the search in everyone to discover their own version of what Jacques Delors called 'the treasure within'[1] is intended to be transformational not just for individuals and whole groups, but for social processes and the operation of institutions themselves. Lifelong learning is deliberately intended to be challenging, difficult and liable to call into question much established policy and practice. Far from being all 'motherhood and apple pie', as so often contended by its critics and even by some of its friends, the real character of lifelong learning is likely to be subversive, critical and disputatious. What is more, in many respects that has to be its explicit purpose, if it is genuinely to contribute to fundamental change in our society and to alter radically the role, form and outcomes of our system of education, especially our schools.

Lifelong learning is rarely talked about in this fashion. After all, to do so is to risk either its wholesale rejection or else its being accused of throwing overboard all the other positive reforms that have been accomplished through much pain and struggle over recent years. Raising the profile of lifelong learning as a critique of much that we already do, by way of schooling, education and training, might be expected to warn off some potential allies, as well as many of its recently won fair weather friends. These have been persuaded that taking on lifelong learning will enable them better to achieve the goals and priorities they have already set, without requiring them to re-think or re-order their established aims and activities. Understandably, contentious and uncomfortable notions of lifelong learning will not be welcome, least of all perhaps in the world of education, including schools, unless its wider advantages are spelled out convincingly.

Putting schools at the centre

So, where to begin, from the point of view of schools and schooling? First, and perhaps most important, lifelong learning cannot be thought of as something that occurs only after, outside and beyond school. Of course, it will be all of those things but the nature of all of them will be changed and enhanced too if lifelong learning is conceived of as a central element of school life. This means that lifelong learning must not be thought of principally as a 'post-sixteen' matter, as it still largely is within the context of British educational policy and practice. If lifelong learning is left until sixteen and beyond, inevitably many young adults will already have been severely disadvantaged educationally and many will be inclined to reject the world of learning which, so far after all, has served too may of them relatively ill. Young adults' attitudes, aspirations, values and orientations will already have been shaped by their childhood experiences of school and other settings. If these have lead them to turn their backs on the uninspiring prospects of yet more learning in adulthood, then no amount of well-intentioned persuasion or even of imposition will win them to a positive frame of mind. And who could blame them, if engagement with learning so far has meant failure, boredom, loss of self-esteem, irrelevance, ridicule and absence of pleasure and fun?

Even those bravely prepared to take advantage of so-called 'second chance' education, by seeking to remedy the failings of their earlier exposure to school through subsequent 'lifelong learning' will not be entirely spared

the unavoidable stench of condescension that accompanies much 'remedial' post-school provision, however well-intentioned or successful. Theirs is a loss that no amount of compensatory provision beyond school can ever fully remedy and, truth to tell, much of it does little to identify the real cause of that original loss in the processes and practices of schooling itself. They are just as likely to put their earlier lack of interest or success down to their own shortcomings alone, or to some accident of background or circumstance. This is not an argument for the abolition or restriction of such 'second chance' provision, but a desire for it too to change in its relation to initial education.

So, schools themselves must embrace lifelong learning as a primary and continuing responsibility. What more would that mean? Most of all, it would mean equipping schools, teachers and parents to be able to develop and enrich in children a love of learning and a sense of continuing pleasure in its processes, outcomes and achievements. These are challenging tasks and will not be accomplished unless, at the same time, the realms and fields in which children can find expressions of their own excellence are substantially diversified. This should not be done by lowering standards in a uniform and homogeneous arena of achievement, just in order to provide a bogus and patronising sense of success for all. That would be disastrous and would rightly attract opprobrium from all sides. Such a radical shift can only be brought about through a genuine multiplication of the forms and manifestations of excellence, and of the various routes to achieving it. The early tyrannies of academic hegemony, unhelpful abstraction and fiercely age-related accomplishments (or failures) at school are too often the root cause of adult indifference or hostility to learning. Moreover, they are also often a poor introduction to the multi-faceted conceptions of excellence, success, achievement and value in adult life.

This is a profoundly difficult issue for academically oriented and successful policy makers, parents and public commentators to grasp. Even many of those who strive genuinely to act on what they take to be its implications are inclined to believe that it is enough to call for 'parity of esteem' between, for example, vocational and academic qualifications. And yet, they continue to despair at the apparent dogged resistance of established hierarchies of judgement of children's achievements and rightly condemn the social sorting which normally accompanies it. Turning this round will mean establishing a much more plural set of values where schooling is concerned and resourcing schools and teachers properly to implement and support a diversity of types and levels of attainment.

If more fields of endeavour and a greater range of talents are to be recognised amongst school children, appropriate and stretching standards will need to be established in all of these arenas. Nobody will be grateful in the long run, including the children themselves (either in childhood or later), for the setting of less demanding targets in so-called 'non-academic' subjects, or even for defining them principally in relation to what they are not! Even more challenging will be the sensitive task of suiting every child's learning environment to that child's own particular needs and developing positive attitudes, including the setting of appropriate goals and what would convey a real sense of genuine achievement. However, if equal opportunities at school are to be fully implemented, children with a wide range of abilities and disabilities must all be enabled to achieve their best. This is not least in order to excite and support their own self-advocacy of those continuing rights and the maintenance of those self-same personal responsibilities in adulthood.

Teachers will rightly point out that many of them entered teaching with precisely these laudable ambitions in mind. What currently thwarts them, they will justifiably argue, are the insistent and narrow demands of politicians, inspectors, parents, employers and the press and the sheer lack of resources. In a world where schools and teachers continue to be judged against conventional and limiting criteria, where crude 'league tables' dominate and the rewards go to those schools and pupils who succeed according to prevailing standards, all such talk of broadening conceptions of excellence at school is largely impractical idealism. So, achieving these changes for schools will require simultaneous action on many fronts. Not least, it will need powerful advocacy by policy makers who are prepared to make a stand to explain and support the case for a much richer and more nuanced conception of schooling excellence, including but not restricted to the achievement of basic and key skills for all.

But, the required changes in attitude and recognition cannot be expected to take place at the level of schools alone. If the world of employment continues to confer the highest status and rewards on those who demonstrate high achievement according to currently conventional criteria of successful schooling, it will not be enough to diversify excellence at school and legitimate varieties of accomplishment. Despite the claimed desires of employers to the contrary, high academic status and achievement still attract their highest ratings, as analysis of their recruitment practices amongst the young reveals.

Learning to learn

Diversifying the curriculum and the terrain of accomplishment will also require shifts in pedagogy and methods of learning and teaching. But, more than this, if adults themselves are to be able to continue to avail themselves of a rapidly expanding world of information and knowledge, they will need to acquire as children the skills and aptitudes to facilitate this. Knowing how to know, understanding how to understand and learning how to learn are at the heart of the key skills for lifelong learning, as the Campaign for Learning is showing. Of course, some vital baseline knowledge and foundational understandings will continue to be essential for subsequent learning: to argue otherwise will be absurd. But so quickly is the scale and relevance of information now changing, that nobody can expect to absorb sufficient at the outset of their learning to see them through life successfully.

Learning to learn is not just a matter of mastering some useful study skills, although these are a vital element of that capacity. Learning to learn is also about developing a set of attitudes, orientations and mentalities about knowledge and information. It includes knowing how to handle all sorts of information and how to process data, how to evaluate competing interpretations and claims and what deductions and conclusions may reasonably be drawn from given information. Learning to learn crucially includes learning how to think both critically and imaginatively, using varieties of resources and different sorts of background information and evaluative criteria. Learning to learn extends to developing people's capacity for imagination and their grasp of alternative perspectives and time frames. It is essentially about training the mind to be open to a range of possibilities, including through intellectual play and inventiveness, as well as through the rigorous application of logic and use of robust criteria of proof.

Learning to learn enables people to know how and where and when to seek information and what to do with the knowledge obtained. It also extends to the application and practical implementation of knowledge, where understanding gives rise to empirical manifestation. This includes acquiring the capacity for imaginative prefiguring of a variety of possible outcomes and scenarios and understanding the consequences of turning knowledge and information into action.

Teachers and parents, too

But, if these exciting and demanding skills are to become a normal part of schooling for all, it will also be necessary to equip the teachers to be able to instil them, and others, in the children. Creating a range of orientations to lifelong learning from early schooldays onwards will embrace the stimulation of a love of learning in children because of the different benefits, joys, pleasures and accomplishments it can manifestly bring them. If teachers are to be able to convey these values and foster these approaches to learning, we shall need to provide for their own lifelong learning and to broaden their own commitment to their continuing development and their shared responsibility for it. This should include not only their own continued professional development, to keep up with the demands of their occupation, but also opportunities for their own cultural, aesthetic, physical and social wellbeing and activities. Thus, teachers will also be able to act as role models for their pupils as much as anything in manifesting and validating a variety of forms and arenas of learning throughout life.

None of this will be accomplished without introducing other changes where teachers are concerned and there will be additional costs to meet as well. Those cannot and should not be denied, even if there will be additional benefits as a consequence. Teacher training programmes, and the skills of those teaching the teachers, will have to be modified, to include the preparation of trainee teachers both for their own lifelong learning and to be able successfully to develop the skills, aptitudes and attitudes for lifelong learning in their future pupils. There will be implications for staffing ratios and for the creation of appropriately mixed teams of professionals to work together in the classrooms of the future. Physical resources will need to be diversified and teachers will be required to learn not only how to manage these efficiently but, above all, how to become the effective managers of learning, that is of learners, of learning environments and of learning support teams.

Within the realm of learning support, parents will also need to be given the confidence and capability to encourage their children's learning and also to continue their own, sometimes alongside or in partnership with their children. For this they will need time, opportunity, resources and, most of all, positive feelings about themselves and a sense of self-esteem enhanced through

learning. Just how far from this many parents still are is easy to imagine, bearing in mind their own experience of school and their often bitterly remembered experiences of shame, shortcoming and inadequacy. Many of them still suffer such feelings as parents, in their inability to understand their own children's schooling or to lend some assistance at home to their children's learning. For them, unlike their much more confident peers, the very thought of entering the school (especially uninvited or unsummonsed) induces anxiety and an unwarranted sense of willing deference to the professionals working there. In such circumstances currently, parents' evenings can so easily become occasions of great stress all round, of insufficient consideration, of inadequate communication and, frankly, of little practical value. And all of this usually in the absence of the very people who are the principal subjects and supposed beneficiaries of the often stilted conversations, the children themselves! Many teachers have themselves been inadequately prepared for working with parents, including not only in their capacities as parents of the schools' children, but also as adults with their own learning needs and interests.

Against this, if only they could be so mobilised as to support the whole of the school and the varied learning activities of all of the children, the voluntary contributions of parents to the vitality and exuberance of schools could be truly transformatory. The adults in a community would, so often, be able to draw upon a rich diversity of skills, experiences, knowledge and competences. Put at the disposal of the whole of the school and under the trained guidance and management of teachers prepared for such work, the resources of schools could be significantly enhanced and at little direct cost.

Schools as centres of lifelong learning

From there, it is only a short step to think imaginatively of schools as a key physical, social and intellectual resource for neighbourhoods, indeed as the natural centres of local, community and lifelong learning. This is where resources for adult, distance, continuing and electronic learning should be located, bringing the undoubted advantages of accessibility, economies of scale and the potential for building learning into life and making it utterly normal for everyone. Again, of course, such developments could not easily occur without other concurrent shifts being at least mooted by those involved, if not thought of as essential, for the ultimate success of the proposed endeavour.

If neighbourhoods and local communities are to be given the chance to make such enhanced contributions to learning at school and to use schools much more to support their own learning, they will probably wish to exert more direct influence over the life of the school. Matters as diverse as schools governance, resource allocation, strategic development, performance review, investment and hours of opening may all need to be opened up to wider consideration and debate. And people will also need the skills and outlooks to be able to handle these new social arrangements, especially the interface between professionals and other members of the local community.

There will be many practical issues to consider, as well as matters of policy and educational practice. Greater local autonomy and involvement will have to be achieved alongside continuing respect for national standards and priorities in fields as diverse as school targets and pay and conditions of work. There will also be the tricky and unavoidable matter of ensuring that schools organised along the lines advocated here do not simply become the educational reinforcements and legitimations of other inequalities between and within local neighbourhoods. Someone will therefore need to have the responsibility and authority for allocating resources and providing other support to such schools according to need, and agreement will be required on the criteria for fair allocations.

This is no easy agenda, and the scale of the changes required to secure its implementation has been only initially addressed in this short chapter. The developments advocated here will take time, leadership, determination, courage and resources to accomplish. But the rewards of moving schools to the centre of the lifelong learning stage will far outweigh its costs. The consequential benefits will be felt, not only throughout life but also across many of its dimensions. Such changes will contribute crucially, too, to making learning increasingly lifewide as well as lifelong.

---

[1] Jacques Delors, *Learning: The Treasure within,* UNESCO, 1966

Learning and Work

Tom Bewick

"We must move away from a view of education as a rite of passage involving the acquisition of enough knowledge and qualifications to acquire an adult station in life. The point of education should not be to inculcate a body of knowledge, but to develop capabilities: the basic ones of literacy and numeracy as well as the capability to act responsibly towards others, to take initiative and to work creatively and collaboratively. The most important capability and one which traditional education is worst at creating is the ability and yearning to carry on learning. Too much schooling kills off a desire to learn".

Charles Leadbeater, *Living on thin air.* [1]

THE BEST TIME OF OUR LIVES, WE ARE TOLD, are our school days. A time for opportunity that will lead to the life chances not yet realised. At the age of six, it is remarkable how pupils describe a vision of themselves in adulthood in such precise occupational terms.

Observe any primary school classroom today, and you will find children that say they want to be nurses, doctors, teachers, fire fighters, pilots, secretaries, engineers, and more recently, software engineers, internet web designers and environmental workers. Their aspirations are enhanced by school trips to large factories, museums and farmyards where the excitement of the extra-curricula world that exists beyond the classroom will be the only encounter many young children will have with employers until they leave full-time education.

So it is perhaps not surprising that by the age of 16, after 10,000 hours of formal schooling, that most young people will cease describing their future destinations in such vocational or work-related terms. How is it that an insatiable desire to achieve an occupational status as expressed in the first stages of childhood has turned, by the coming of age, into an inevitable expectation that 'staying on' in full-time education is the only option?

Staying on is not inherently a bad thing. Double the amount of 17 years-olds gain A-levels compared to 10 years ago. The number of enrolments in sixth forms and Further Education has increased by 28 per cent since 1994. It is the mark of all highly developed societies that, as the complex processes of production and information communication technologies demand new forms of work and social organisation, the general level of academic attainment has risen significantly. The more difficult issue to address, however, is whether such exponential demand for 'more learning' has to be met within the confines of existing institutional and qualification arrangements.

There are also more subtle forces to be addressed. Arguably, too many of our young people are encouraged by a pervasive, predominantly middle class culture of, 'staying-on'. The main influences are parents, teachers, careers advisers and politicians. They help enforce a belief in teenagers that five GCSEs, a clutch of A-levels and a university degree is the best route to future success. For a significant minority of young people who fail to reach these levels of academic attainment, they are left to take what is culturally re-enforced as a second rate option for advancement in further learning and the labour market. And, while work-based training and apprenticeships have recovered from the rock-bottom reputation that YTS had among employers and young people in the 1980s, the so called 'work-based route' is currently neither understood nor promoted in schools in anything like the way it should.

These are issues that go to the heart of any serious debate about the future relationship between school and the workplace. How do we adequately prepare young people for fulfilling, creative and rewarding lives, in the internet age, as opposed to the continuation of policies that have more in common with a bygone age?

This chapter briefly explores the relationship between learning and work. It highlights that a major problem with our compulsory education system is that it has historically erected a whole array of barriers to exclude employers in the organisation and delivery of the school curriculum, when partnership could have been more mutually beneficial. Against this context, a changing economy, relying on new occupational roles in ways not dreamt of a generation ago, demands new thinking about the choices young people are encouraged to make.

The final part of the chapter looks at current developments in policy and proposes further measures to ensure young people are given the broadest learning choices at school and in the workplace. This includes

a controversial proposal to take away the funding and responsibility for secondary schools from LEAs, handing responsibility instead to the new local Learning and Skills Councils (LSCs), which will be responsible for funding all post-16 provision and developing education business links from April 2001. Furthermore, requiring schools and colleges to publish more meaningful employment and earnings related data, is another radical proposal to better inform the learning choices of parents and children.

There are a number of challenges for employers too. A key one is reconciling the drift of current policy to increase young people's participation at both tertiary and higher education level in terms of both the immediate and long-term skill needs of the economy, particularly at intermediate and craft level. This challenge is made more urgent by a demographic fall in the number of 7 to 19 year-olds.

School and workplace: historical barriers to partnership

There are many competing accounts of the history of education. But one plausible explanation for the extension of compulsory schooling was that it was a move, in part, to curb the excesses of nineteenth century capitalism.[2] From the Liberal Government's perspective of the late 1800s, these extremes were as much borne out by a fear of political upheaval, as they were recognition that the state should intervene to improve the living conditions of the general population. This was a view shared by the other dominant political force at the time. For senior Conservatives like Arthur Balfour the march of social legislation was, *"not merely to be distinguished from socialist legislation, but it is its most direct opposite and its most effective antidote".²*

In the hey-day of British dominance of manufacturing and world-trade, other less political considerations were evident. Domestic manufacturers were under pressure from foreign competitors who thought Britain's claim to be the 'workshop of the world' was increasingly overstated. The Victorian appetite for socio-economic inquiries on a pavlovian scale, further re-enforced a view that the pride of the nation was under attack from all sides. This manifested itself in the emerging ideological battleground of education.

Forster's Act of 1870 extended elementary education and is an early example of the politician's desire to win over the business community. Enacted before the horrors of the war in South Africa, Forster argued in the House of Commons,

"the speedy provision of elementary education depends on industrial prosperity. It is no use trying to give technical teaching to our artisans without elementary education".³

Despite a growing awareness that other industrial competitors were already overtaking Britain, there was major complaint from employers that such heavy handed intervention by the state would seriously restrict the supply of labour into the rising smoke-stacks and sweatshops of England. The intemperate, and some might say, myopic attitudes of leading industrialists gave employers a bad name in the eyes of an emerging teaching profession who viewed with suspicion the merchant's desire for 'factory fodder'.

By the time Fisher's Education Act had extended secondary compulsory education to fourteen in 1902, the historical barriers to partnership between school and the workplace were firmly established. This most acutely embodied itself in the emerging role of the new Local Education Authorities (LEAs), who perceived themselves as the custodians of 'moral education' and enlightenment and guarded jealously against any attempts by industry to subvert the curriculum or, indeed, the orderly running of schools. This was re-enforced, of course, by the established church which had since the Dark Ages provided education as a means of refuge and recruitment to the ecclesiastical orders.

And so the historical demarcation between learning and work took root. While teachers were left alone to run the inner-sanctity of the new Victorian-built school-houses, employers were left to get on running the dark, satanic mills depicted in the vivid nineteenth century novels of Charles Dickens.

Toward a new partnership

Great strides may not have been achieved in the last 100 years, but the dividing lines between the worlds of education and work are at last beginning to be addressed, as 21st century communities grapple with globalisation and the 'new economy'. A new economy in which the asset base is shifting away from the tangible goods that can be weighed at the ports in kilos and tonnes, to the intangible assets of knowledge which are tied up in the brains and ingenuity of all our people.

Although often overstated, the changing economy is helping to forge a renewed climate of trust and mutual reconciliation between the educational establishment and the business community. Nowhere is this more evident than in the multi-racial and enterprise culture of the United States, where employers have a long track record in working with local communities to set up and administer schools. Some schools in American cities, often re-named 'learning centres' or technology, sports and music 'academies' are organised like some of the most progressive enterprises; where flexitime, team-building, mentors and subject learning equates to multi-skilling and a flexible curriculum.

Britain has also developed innovate ways of engaging business in the running of schools. The number of specialist schools, with the strong backing of local employers, has doubled in recent years. There will be over 800 specialist schools in existence, nearly one in four of all secondary schools, by 2004. Specialist schools, like many of the schools in the Government's assigned Education Action Zones are set up in partnership with business, and aim not only to raise standards in academic education but also encourage diversity in the curriculum representing a strong under-current of 'vocationalism'. This has been particularly successful in the case of some football league clubs, many of whom are global businesses, who have re-engaged a number of mainly young boys in learning by offering IT and after-school homework centres in conjunction with football coaching and mentoring.

Despite the apparent progress in closer partnerships between school and the workplace, there is still a widespread belief that the best role for employers is to contribute from afar. This may explain why so many businesses are approached each year to sponsor or buy the school minibus, equip an IT centre or provide work placements to young people that are rarely formally evaluated by the school in terms of their contribution to the overall attainment of pupils. A real challenge in this on-going debate, therefore, will be the degree to which employers are really encouraged to actively help shape the lives of young people over the next few years.

More informed choice

One area where more employer involvement is critical is in helping to better inform the career choices of young people. The acclaimed university fellow, John Berkeley, highlights the problem in a study of GNVQs for 14-16 year-olds. Looking at the aspirations of those taking the engineering course and the advice that they received from teachers and others, he found that despite having chosen a highly practical, vocational course, most were strongly advised to stay on at school for 'A'-Levels. A significant number would have preferred to leave school at 16 to pursue an apprenticeship, but were persuaded otherwise, according to Berkeley, by teachers and parents alike.[4]

Similarly, in a survey of 200 Rover trainees, only a quarter had been advised by their school to apply for an apprenticeship or other work-based training. Better careers advice and impartial guidance to pupils at age eleven upwards is critical if we are to break the 'default culture' of staying on in full-time education. The funding of schools, and sixth-forms in particular, currently mitigates against this happening. Head teachers are responsible for both managing impartial careers advice, and ensuring that the numbers transferring from fifth to sixth-form or the local college add up each year in order to balance the books. It is a system in which schools are allowed to operate as poacher and game-keeper, a sort of cartel that needs to be broken up if we are serious about making available more informed choices for all our young people.

The National Skills Task Force neatly summed up this debate and have tackled the issue head on in their final report to government:

> "The learning choices young people make in school at ages 13 to 14 can significantly shape the career choices available to them later. We must therefore start to inform choice early. Young people should receive structured careers education and project-based preparation for the labour market from age 12 onwards. From age 14; all schools should introduce quality academic and vocational options for all young people, work experience and careers guidance should focus on helping young people to begin to identify potential career choices. It is also essential that such provision seeks to inform parents, too, as they have such an influential role on their children's decisions."[5]

One way for these decisions to be better informed, will be through a much closer co-operation between the intelligence gathering of National Training Organisations (NTOs), and the application of this intelligence by guidance services such as the new Connexions service, which will offer comprehensive advice and support to young people in England. NTOs, as employer organisations, have a responsibility to assess the skills needs of a particular occupational or industrial sector. NTOs are sitting on a wealth of information about the demand for skills, the demands of job roles and the career learning paths available to cater for a wide range of abilities. This plethora of information

is yet to be turned into real intelligence. But in a few sectors, there has been the development of sophisticated on-line learning resources and guidance tools explaining everything from how many recruits are needed each year in the sector, to pay rates and long-term career prospects. These developments could really transform the learning choices of teenagers if properly used by guidance professionals and teachers in schools.

Reconciling academic drift with the skills agenda

At the moment there appears to be a contradiction in the Government's desire for more young people in further and higher-education on the one hand, and a laudable belief in greater 'parity of esteem' between the academic and work-based route on the other. It is particularly noticeable in the difference of approach between the Secretary of State, David Blunkett, who talks of a new 'vocational ladder' in 14-19 education and the Chancellor, Gordon Brown, who insists on talking the language of "staying on at school". There is danger in his pronouncements, in particular, that we become seduced by the soothing words of academic drift: a schism at the heart of government policy that may have serious ramifications for meeting the long-term needs of both business and the economy.

A major survey carried out by the Government's Skills Task Force found that 40 per cent of all skills shortages are in craft and technician type jobs, requiring high-level skills gained through substantial job-specific, work-based training.[6] There is also evidence that industry will require an increasing supply of young people at level 3 or equivalent if we are to plug the gap at the intermediate level that exists between ourselves and other industrialised countries, notably Germany.[7]

David Blunkett's answer to the problem has been the introduction of vocational GCSEs, vocational A-levels and foundation degrees. The Chancellor appears more ambivalent. He has set specific targets in his Comprehensive Spending Review for the "majority of young people to enter higher education by 2010", 60 per cent of 21-year-olds to have A-levels by 2004 and an extra 80,000 more 16-18 year olds in full-time college from 2004. This will occur at a time when the number of young people in the labour force will be dropping due to historically low birth rates. In 1981, 9.9 per cent of the labour force were aged 16-19; by 1994, this had fallen to 5.8 per cent.[8]

The Treasury's recent target fetishism for increasing levels of academic participation is even more alarming when they are viewed against the context of one of the lowest levels of public investment in workplace apprenticeships in Western Europe. The average EU member state, for example, spends 2 per cent of GDP on work-based apprenticeships, whereas Britain spends under 1 per cent.[9]

History has a habit of repeating itself. The echoes of the debate surrounding Forster's Education Act all those years ago can still be heard. Skills shortages and the level of technical expertise will worsen unless government is prepared to set more meaningful targets in the arena of vocational education and work-based training. The unified approach to post-16 education and training in England being brought about by the creation of the new national Learning and Skills Council, and its 47 local arms present an considerable opportunity to rectify the false distinctions that have dogged learning and the work-place for decades. The argument is again best illuminated by the work of John Berkeley, who is asking some difficult questions:

"Under the present system, the numbers of apprentices in training has been largely determined by the funding regime. In engineering manufacture, with one of the largest groups of apprentices, we have 21,800 in training at present for a workforce of around 1.7 million. That's a ratio of 1.3 per cent. But is that the right ratio? And what does it conceal? Are there occupations which are well-served with apprentices and others which are dangerously neglected?

"In Germany, by comparison, the position is much clearer. The proportion of apprentices, as a percentage of the total numbers in that occupation, is seen as an important measure. Take agricultural machinery mechanics, for example. With 1,547 apprentices in training in Bavaria and for a workforce of 6,786, the ratio is high even by German standards, at 22.8 per cent. In England and Wales, the corresponding ratio is 0.29 per cent with 170 apprentices in training. To take another example, apprentice plumbers in Bavaria represent 14.6 per cent of adult workers. Here, the ratio appears to be under 1 per cent."[10]

We have no systematic way in Britain of knowing whether particular industries or occupations are well served by the foundation learning and apprenticeship system. NTOs provide a sectoral dimension, but too many are under-resourced to tackle the job in hand effectively. Too much of the debate about training performance takes place at the level of generality and often misses the point, in terms of addressing specific issues that affect different types of employment sectors and occupations. The Confederation of British Industry is over-reliant on the thesis that views the deficiencies of the UK's skills base as the problem of an inadequate schooling system which, of course, is seen as an issue for government to resolve.

The under-achievement in the workforce, including the seven million adults lacking basic skills is also perceived in terms of being primarily a government responsibility. In future, the solutions to these skills issues will need to be far less one-sided. Government, individuals, communities and especially employers hold the key to a better education and training system all round. The Skills Task Force recommendation, to provide level two and three learning entitlements to all young people and adults is the right solution, but it cannot be realised through public funding alone. Employers have also to contribute and invest adequately in the skills of this group in particular. It is a fact that employers are spending more on training now than ever, but it is also true that this investment is spent on those already rich in skills, qualifications and life chances. People with a degree are four times more likely to receive training from their employer than those without qualifications. This comes at a time when the number of training days, according to the Labour Force Survey, has fallen from five in 1996 to three in 1998.

The challenge to employers

Employers need to change their entrenched attitudes toward the youth labour market and apprenticeship system – if only to avoid a potential recruitment, entry and intermediate level skills crisis in future. Britain suffers from a stop-go training cycle: the immediate short-term needs of some industries are falsely traded off against the long-term needs of individual employability and long-term competitiveness. For example, over 40 per cent of Modern Apprentices fail to complete the full framework. In some cases they simply drift back to full-time education or in the worst case scenario, unemployment or even social exclusion.

But there are also cases where employers entice young people off the Government-supported programmes to meet more short-term business needs. Only a minority of the NTO frameworks for modern apprenticeships, for example, specify any requirement for formal vocational education or off-the-job training. Of course, policy makers need to respect the fact that some sectors of industry have no need for such requirements, but we must equally be on our guard against the quality of the apprenticeship experience being undermined by employers who are unwilling to invest for the long-term.

Employers must, in particular, develop new ways of securing the confidence of parents and school leavers, persuading them that work-based learning pays, and is regarded just as highly in the eyes of managers and parents as traditional academic qualifications. Employers need to influence this debate long before the statutory school leaving age. Relying on the hoards of unqualified school leavers that once helped fill the twilight jobs now popular with students and overseas workers is simply not a sustainable way forward.

Replacing LEAs with LSCs

One way that employers and the business community could be more engaged in England's 24,000 schools, is through the local Learning and Skills Councils (LSCs). These bodies will have a statutory duty to support Education Business Partnerships (EBPs), which are to attract more substantial public funding for the first time. But this may also be the time to think more radically about the future management and delivery of secondary and post-compulsory education.

In a major speech at the Cranfield School of Management, in September 2000, the Prime

Minister captured the headlines with a call for the shake-up of comprehensive education. It was difficult to decipher exactly what he meant. Modernisation and greater diversity are platitudes if they give very little away in terms of what actual forms of delivery are needed. The lack of any reference to the future role of Local Education Authorities was also conspicuous by its absence. What is the role of the LEA in this future education revolution? Already, we have seen central government send more and more resources directly to schools. LEAs have reserved for themselves a strategic planning function for essential services, such as school meals, libraries and special needs education, but there are a few cases where even this role has been contracted-out to private enterprise.

The demise of the Local Education Authorities will continue with the arrival of local Learning and Skills Councils. This will only lead to a diminution of local democracy and local control over schools if elected councillors are prevented from serving on LSC boards alongside local employers and other community interests. This should not happen. Furthermore, there are compelling arguments for handing over the funding and responsibility for secondary education to the LSCs. For a start, it would open up the possibility, in times where school-work transition has never been more of a barrier for young people, of a genuinely joined-up and coherent 11-19 education and vocational training strategy.

The existing engagement of business and employers in post-16 learning could be put to good effect in sorting out the overburdened National Curriculum that is increasingly confining pupils and teachers within an academic straight jacket. How else is the Government going to secure employer commitment and a real currency for vocational GCSEs when they are introduced from 2002? If LEAs stay in control, these qualifications will remain the preserve of those seen as 'failing' at school. They need to become the first choice for some highly able young people, as well as a second chance for a considerable number of pupils who become disengaged from the academic curriculum each year.

Future policy

The building blocks of future policy are beginning to take shape. The Government appears committed to a vocational ladder of opportunity from age 14. The Labour Party's draft manifesto for a second term is some indication of what might be to come:

> "More teenagers should benefit from workplace learning and the motivation that follows from it. ... In the revised National Curriculum we will extend flexibility to promote further workplace learning and to encourage young people to develop their special talents and interests".[11]

Future government policy will have to be even more radical if it is to cope with the pace of change. Tom Bentley takes up this challenge in his work at the influential think-tank, Demos:

> "we have a structure where knowledge is transmitted within an institutional context. But our schools are organised in a completely different way to any other institution a person is likely to meet in his or her life. There's widespread recognition that education needs to be seen in a broader sense than the strictly formal to produce a wider set of outcomes for children, such as their ability to become good parents and citizens, but the curriculum has not been adapted to accommodate them".[12]

He proposes to slim down the National Curriculum by half. He also envisages a future for GCSEs and A-levels which are "re-shaped to include far more continuous assessment, that pupils take exams when they are able, not at a certain age, and that the whole shape changed, with far more emphasis on individual and peer assessment".

Another important plank of future policy should be to explore the extent to which certain courses and qualifications pay for the learner. We know a great deal about the general economic returns to higher education. On average, graduates will earn over 40 per cent more in a lifetime than non-graduates earning the average wage. But we know far less about the returns to investment from individual university, college and work-based learning outcomes. This will have to change in future, if consumers of learning are to benefit from a more demand-led and responsive approach. Colleges, training providers and universities, particularly those offering the new foundation degrees, should be required to publish information about the job and earnings potential of particular learning choices. Over time, some proportion of funding should be provided to institutions on the basis of how well they gain sustainable employment outcomes for their former students.

Conclusion

Overcoming the historical divides between learning and work is still a very real challenge for pupils, parents and policy-makers alike. The challenge for schools over the next few years will be to become more 'open institutions' in the way that they relate to employers and the wider community.

This is not only because industry and the occupations we do not yet know exist will require future workers that are well equipped to meet the economy's growing needs. The whole nature of learning and the acquisition of knowledge in our society is changing. Gone are the days when schooling itself could be relied upon as an adequate preparation for adult life. As Charles Leadbeater warns at the beginning of this chapter, "too much schooling kills off a desire to learn". If we are serious about developing a culture of continuous lifelong learning, then learning at school and learning for the workplace will need to become far more synonymous with one another than has hitherto been the case. This is the inevitable consequence of the history that is now unfolding before us.

[1] Charles Leadbeater, *Living on thin air: the new economy*, Viking, 1999

[2] A. M. Rees. *T. H. Marshall's Social Policy*, Hutchinson, 1985

[3] Quoted in *Education at work: a report prepared by the Employment Policy Institute for Edexcel, Edexcel*, 2000

[4] John Berkeley OBE *Learning for Work: Time for a Change?*, speech given to the Learning and Skills Council Conference, supported by FEDA, Unemployment Unit, NTO National Council, 2000

[5] *Skills for all: proposals for a national skills agenda*, National Skills Task Force, 2000

[6] *Skills for all:* research project report from the National Skills Task Force, DfEE, 2000

[7] *Fact not fiction: UK training performance*, CBI, July 2000

[8] *Jobless figures affected by fall in young people*, Financial Times, 7 August 2000.

[9] *Training in the global economy*, International Labour Organisation, 1999

[10] John Berkeley, *Learning for Work: Time for a Change?*, Speech as [4] above

[11] *Building a future for all: national policy forum reports to conference*, Labour Party, September 2000.

[12] Quoted in The Guardian, *A new look at learning*, Guardian Education, 28 March 2000.

Citizenship schools: the new learning revolution

Titus Alexander

THE NEW NATIONAL CURRICULUM FOR citizenship is more than another subject to be squeezed into an overcrowded timetable. It is an approach to education that offers schools an opportunity to renew themselves from the bottom up and meet the immense challenges of the twenty-first century.

This chapter looks at a double barrelled challenge confronting schools – unremitting external pressures for better performance, and the need to introduce a whole new subject, citizenship education, from September 2002. To meet both challenges, schools should involve pupils, parents and staff in a careful process of educational renewal to create what I call 'citizenship schools'.

Almost two decades ago, in *The Challenge for the Comprehensive School,* David Hargreaves wrote:

"*After the upheavals of the last twenty years many teachers would clearly like a quiet period of consolidation, but most know only too well that this will not be provided. On the contrary, yet more changes are likely to come, and many of these … will bring yet further problems and burdens for teachers".*[1]

As they did. Hargreaves urged the teaching profession to: "take a stronger initiative in participating in the design of future reform" and "a more active role in determining the shape of the relationship between education and society". For this "teachers will have to acquire a set of skills which the vast majority now lack – political skills". If they do not, "the alternative is quite clear: they will continue to be told what to do, the message will be critical and contradictory, and they will be forced back yet further into a defensive and burdensome position". And so they were.

For Hargreaves, the response to constant change was not defensive politics, but the "difficult task of creating a comprehensive curriculum which … meets the full range of needs and talents of all children". As the pressures on schools continues unabated, the challenge remains.

Schools throughout the country – and the world – are exploring these same issues and developing different ways of dealing with them. For many, these pressures are a challenge. They are answering fundamental questions about education in new ways. Some of the practical solutions they have come up with are described in the second part of this article. But first it is worth reminding ourselves of the purpose of the new national curriculum.

Citizenship and the purpose of learning

For the first time ever, the national curriculum provides a statement of values and purpose for education.[2] The revised statement is worthy and rather wordy, with two aims, which are that the school curriculum should:

1. Develop enjoyment of, and commitment to, learning as a means of encouraging and stimulating the best possible progress and the highest attainment for all pupils.
2. Promote pupils' spiritual, moral, social and cultural development and prepare all pupils for the opportunities, responsibilities and experiences of life, and, in particular, develop principles for distinguishing between right and wrong.

Perhaps more important is the statement of purpose for education, which includes the following statements:

"Foremost is a belief in education, at home and at school as a route to the spiritual, moral, social, cultural, physical and mental development, and thus the well-being, of the individual.

Education is also a route to equality of opportunity for all, a healthy and just democracy, a productive economy, and sustainable development.

Education should reflect the enduring values that contribute to these ends. These include valuing ourselves, our families and other relationships, the wider groups to which we belong, the diversity in our society and the environment in which we live.

Education should also reaffirm our commitment to the virtues of truth, justice, honesty, trust and a sense of duty.

At the same time, education must enable us to respond positively to the opportunities and challenges of the rapidly changing world in which we live and work. In particular, we need

to be prepared to engage as individuals, parents, workers and citizens with economic, social and cultural change, including the continued globalisation of the economy and society, with new work and leisure patterns and with the rapid expansion of communication technologies".

These aims put the world, personal development and responsible citizenship at the centre of education, not the curriculum. They express a vision for society and the role of education within it. Although, in practice, teachers and inspectors may treat the curriculum as the subject of education, it is only a means to learning in a rapidly changing world. The full statement of aims and purpose could be summarised in three lines:

to develop the skills, knowledge, understanding and values for personal well-being as active and responsible citizens in a changing world.

The new national curriculum is clear that citizenship and personal development are integral to the whole purpose of education, not just an additional subject alongside others. But it is not yet clear whether the Government itself has assimilated the full potential of its own curriculum.

Tensions in government policy
The curriculum itself cannot remain static," as the QCA acknowledges.

"It must be responsive to changes in society and the economy, and changes in the nature of schooling itself. Teachers, individually and collectively, have to reappraise their teaching in response to the changing needs of their pupils and the ideas and attitudes of society and economic forces. Education only flourishes if it successfully adapts to the demands and needs of the time".[3]

This highlights an acute tension at the centre of government education policy. The best learning is about people thinking for themselves, following their curiosity, discovering new things, and developing competence with words, numbers, books, science, technology and people as they do so. But education is compulsory, the curriculum is laid down by statute, school life is closely supervised by inspection and even teaching methods are increasingly directed from the centre. Politicians, education officials and head teachers anxious about targets bear down on schools, teachers, pupils and parents who appear to be under-performing. The ability of teachers and learners to influence what and how they learn feels heavily constrained.

But if the QCA and ministers have made a mistake about what and how people need to learn for life in the twenty-first century, we will all suffer system failure. Indeed, it could be argued that what has happened to schooling over the past century is precisely that: system failure.

If schools can show that they are capable of meeting the multiple challenges of learning in a changing world and of building social cohesion as active participants in their local community, as many schools do, they will also be able to make the political case for better funding. Citizenship education is as much about the place of schools in society as about the content of the curriculum.

Enabling young people to "respond positively to the opportunities and challenges of the rapidly changing world" is one of the most important tasks of any society. But what do schools do when the rate of change is so rapid that the future is unknown and unknowable?

Confidence in speaking, reading, writing and number are vital foundations for living and lifelong learning. But attainment will only rise if young people really want to learn what is offered. Even then, high attainment will be irrelevant if they need different skills in the uncharted times beyond school: how much of today's curriculum will matter in 2016, when some of today's reception classes may start to earn a living? The world has already changed enormously since 1984, when today's school leavers started, and the pace of change is accelerating. What if success comes to those who develop distinctive talents during truancy, not the stars of SATs, GCSEs and NVQs? What if today's successful schools, with their well-ordered environments and carefully planned timetables, actually prevent people from making the most of opportunities in the chaos and uncertainty of the future? What if the rascals, pranksters and tearaways make the running in 2020, while the dutiful swots who sacrificed their youth at the alter of assessment are redundant, or consigned to routine low-paid work at the margins of tomorrow's economy? What if the future rewards creative defiance above obedient achievement? The truth is we cannot know.

My guess is the skills for tomorrow are likely to include independence of mind, the ability to form relationships and work with others, skill at solving problems for which there is no right answer and, perhaps, the bloody mindedness to persist when others think you are wrong. What is certain is that most people will need to be effective learners, capable of changing what they do many times during their lives. This means equipping young people to take part in creating their own future, as active participants in their own future. They are not objects of teaching, who must be made to fit into society, but subjects of their own learning, actively contributing to a society which they are also creating as members of a school and local community.

If young people are treated as citizens, responsible for their own learning, in a society of lifelong learners, who share responsibility for the school community and the world, our whole approach to schools becomes very different.

Citizenship and the curriculum

Under our present system, the point of learning is, in practice, to satisfy as closely as possible the prescriptions of external authorities. Although they might have the right prescription for some pupils, this kind of learning is very different from what people need in a fast changing world.

Resolving the tension between personal autonomy and external authority is central for both personal development and citizenship education. The curriculum content may be prescribed, but its practice must be negotiated and increasingly self-determined or it will be a course in hypocrisy. Personal, social and citizenship skills need to be applied to school life as a whole, or they will create unsustainable tensions between a democratic content and a controlling context.

This means schools cannot be seen as institutions that produce accredited pupils according to targets in a national plan, like a factory. Schools must become democratic learning communities which manage their own affairs and engage with society as learning citizens.

The joy of learning

Play is a child's work. It is how the young of the species learns. Play is also central to the human spirit and learning. Mature play is highly disciplined, like sport, music and other arts. Casual play, like conversation, daydreaming, pub games or gossip, is the glue of everyday life. The essence of play is that it is freely undertaken, in free time, a leisure activity when the necessities of life are looked after. Greek philosophers believed that we become most fully human in free time devoted to self-development. Thus the Greek word for leisure, scholea, gave us 'school'. The Latin Ludus means both play and school.

Freedom is only possible when people have the power to exercise it. This includes the inner confidence as much as external circumstances. Everyone has the right to take part in government, but in practice most do not have the freedom to do so, because they lack the time, skills, knowledge or confidence to do so.

It is not enough to say to someone, learn and you will increase your life chances. The learner needs to know that they have the power to apply their learning and to benefit from it. And if they do not like the conditions under which they learn and live, they need the power to take part in the collective learning process of society, through politics as well as markets.

Raising school standards without empowering learners could increase social exclusion, because it leaves behind all those who do not appreciate the power of learning or lack the circumstances to make learning matter.

But schools are not just instruments of instruction or information channels. Skills and knowledge could be delivered more efficiently and attractively in other ways. The core curriculum of reading, writing and arithmetic can be taught in about a hundred hours to those who are eager to learn. Almost the entire curriculum is available on the internet for those who want to study at home. But the vital part of schools is the concern for understanding, values and behaviour. Living in society requires shared ethics. These can only develop through human relationships.

Going to school is an apprenticeship in citizenship. Just as families and states seek to balance freedom and responsibility within their boundaries, so school communities regulate their own affairs as microcosms of society. Like many families and states, schools can be authoritarian, oppressive, democratic or progressive. This small 'p' political culture of schools needs to be explicit if young people are to develop the practice of citizenship and the power of learning.

Most schools today bring together people from different faiths, denominations, social backgrounds and ethnic origins. This makes schools natural successors to places of worship as a focus for community life, in which community values, experience and knowledge are shared and developed. At present pupils have few rights and many duties. As, under the British constitution, they are subjects rather than citizens.

Elements of a citizenship school

A school which empowers its members as learning citizens could be called a 'citizenship school', in which citizenship is practised as well as taught. Many schools are beginning to develop elements of a 'citizenship school', which include:

1. A democratic constitution and ethos, in which all members of the school community are recognised as learning citizens, with explicit rights and responsibilities, as outlined below.

2. Meaningful responsibilities for all pupils, such as:
   • active involvement in deciding and planning what to learn;
   • participating in peer education;
   • maintaining the physical environment, within the school and its grounds;
   • communicating through a newsletter, radio, video, website or other media;
   • conflict resolution and peer mediation;
   • devising and carrying out projects;
   • undertaking research aimed at school improvement;
   • taking part in appointments of teachers, including the head; and
   • pupil appraisal or evaluation of teaching.

These responsibilities are intertwined with the curriculum and decision-making, outlined in the following two sections.

3. An empowering curriculum which includes active development of a sense of self as a person, learner and agent in the world, exploration of values and purpose in all subjects, thinking skills, learning to learn, emotional literacy, enquiry skills, peer education and mentoring, participation in a campaign or project for change, and political understanding. This includes the statutory framework for personal, social and citizenship education.

4. Active participation in decision-making at all levels. For pupils this means:
   • Learning partners and teams to develop mutual support and confidence;
   • Circle time to develop empathy, relationships and values as well as

resolve problems;
- A pupil council with elected representatives from each class and a meaningful role in all decision-making;
- Pupil representatives on the governing body; and
- Local and national representation by young people in decision-making.

For parents, participation takes place through class meetings (or associations) of all parents of children in each class, meeting two or three times a year to discuss the curriculum, concerns about the class and issues affecting the school, as well as to socialise and support the parents' councils consisting of elected representatives from each class.

These levels of participation would give all young people real experience of decision-making and the issues they face in growing up. In almost all cases these would be real decisions, with real consequences, in which young people would have to seek compromise and consensus among themselves as well as with adults.

Conclusion

We could be at the start of a constitutional revolution based on the transformation of schools into the foundations of a new learning democracy. An economy based on knowledge, information and services can only function if people are flexible, skilful and above all capable of thinking for themselves. Employers know they have to treat people with respect or lose business. In many areas, authoritarian management simply does not work. Leading industries invest in people through staff development, support and sometimes even real empowerment, because their own survival

depends on it. Business now spends a third more than the Government on education and training. Many businesses are now more progressive than the public sector, which is often more hierarchical, bureaucratic and unresponsive to people. Many employers also recognise that a divided, unequal and unjust society is bad for business as well as society.

Schools are ideal institutions in which to learn citizenship in practice. They are relatively self-contained, with a well-defined local membership, relatively clear decision-making structures, and an elected governing body representing all stakeholders apart from pupils (the most important!). Schools now manage their own budget, staff and relationships with other agencies, subject to external inspection, the local authority and national directives.

Learning citizenship in practice means developing the skills of listening, understanding other people and issues, building trust, winning and losing arguments, coming to agreement, communicating, establishing effective relationships and above all, being responsible for making decisions which have real influence in the world, for which we are accountable. These are essential skills in a constantly changing, uncertain world.

Thus the new national curriculum for personal, social and citizenship education offers schools the opportunity to renew and transform themselves from the bottom up. This transformation could be even more important than votes for all and universal education in the last century. By sharing power over learning, schools can spread the excitement and possibilities that learning brings. But this transformation cannot be imposed on schools. It can only happen if teachers, pupils, parents, support staff and local communities seize the opportunities of citizenship education.

When they do, schools will also create new relationships with learners and local communities that change the perception and experience of education. It will give schools, as democratic earning communities, an active role in determining the shape of the relationship between education and society, as advocated by David Hargreaves almost twenty years ago.

---

[1] David Hargreaves, *The Challenge for the Comprehensive School: culture, curriculum and community,* Routledge and Kegan Paul, 1982

[2] *National curriculum,* Qualifications and Curriculum Authority, 2000

[3] *The review of the national curriculum in England: Consultation Materials,* Qualifications and Curriculum Authority, 1999

Creativity in schools and beyond

Ken Robinson

THERE IS A DEEP CONTRADICTION AT THE heart of education. The Government emphasises the vital need to promote creativity, innovation and the full development of human resources. But for many people, current policies and pressures seem custom designed to inhibit these things. In 1997 the Government published its White Paper *Excellence in Schools.*[1] It described education as a vital investment in 'human capital' for the twenty-first century. It argued that one of the problems in education is low expectations of young people's abilities and that it is essential to raise morale, motivation and self-esteem in schools. It is clearly stated that:

> "If we are to prepare successfully for the twenty-first century, we will have to do more than just improve literacy and numeracy skills. We need a broad, flexible and motivating education that recognises the different talents of all children and delivers excellence for everyone."

Repeatedly, the Prime Minister and the Secretary of State have said that education is the Government's top priority. An improved education system, they argue, is vital to enable young people to keep pace with and contribute to a world of rapid economic and cultural change. They are absolutely right in this. At the heart of Government policy they also say is a commitment to developing the full natural resources of all young people and, in particular, their powers of creativity and innovation. These are especially important for two reasons.

The first is so that, as a nation, we can be at leading the edge of the new global economies. The economic impact of the new information technologies is such that economic competitiveness is increasingly dependent on intellectual capacity rather than manual labour. New ideas for new products and services are the lifeblood of the new economies. Developing young people's capacity for original ideas is essential for that reason. But the rate of change on all fronts has other implications. It makes it essential that young people and adults alike are able to adapt to changing circumstances: that they are flexible and can roll with change as well as contribute to it. For both reasons, creativity is at the top of the educational agenda, not only in the United Kingdom but in many countries throughout the world.

The National Advisory Committee for Creative and Cultural Education

This is why in February 1998, David Blunkett, the Secretary of State for Education and Employment, and Chris Smith, the Secretary of State for Culture, Media and Sport, established the National Advisory Committee for Creative and

Cultural Education (NACCCE). This was a groundbreaking move in several ways. It was one of the first major cross-departmental initiatives of the new administration, linking the interests of two departments of state. The NACCCE had links to other Government groups, including the Creative Industries Task Force, and was early evidence of the new Government's commitment to joined up thinking. Second, the Committee brought together a unique grouping of people from a wide range of professional backgrounds and interests in the arts, the sciences, business and from education. The Committee included Professor Susan Greenfield, Sir Harry Kroto, Dawn French, Lenny Henry, Sir Simon Rattle, Jude Kelly, the heads of Carlton Television and Marks and Spencer, Sir Claus Moser, Chair of the Basic Skills Agency, Eric Bolton the former Senior Chief Inspector, and other distinguished educators. It was not, in any recognisable sense, a lobby or special interest group. The very range of its membership indicated how widely felt were the issues it was established to address.

The decision to establish the NACCCE came after an approach to David Blunkett in summer 1997 by myself and Jude Kelly, Director of the West Yorkshire Playhouse and a patron of the Campaign for Learning. We were concerned that the Government was emphasising the importance of creative education but seemed to many people to be doing very little to promote it. The main emphasis of Government policy is on raising standards, conceived in conventional academic terms. In particular, they are pre-occupied with raising standards of literacy and numeracy. Let me say at once that I, and the NACCCE as a whole, fully support the commitment to raising these standards. Who would not? The problem is that the

pursuit of these objectives has threatened others, which are equally important. Since taking office the Government has applied forms of assessment and inspection in schools, and increased levels of prescription in teacher education in ways that seem designed to suppress creativity rather than promote it. Outside schools, other organisations, museums, theatres, galleries, orchestras and others, have a huge amount to offer education. Many already have education programmes, but say they are poorly funded for education and that such work has low priority.

Recognising the dangers, perhaps, David Blunkett and Chris Smith convened the NACCCE with broad terms of reference. They were:

> *"To make recommendations to the Secretaries of State on the creative and cultural development of young people through formal and informal education: to take stock of current provision and to make proposals for principles, policies and practice."*

Our report, *All Our Futures: Creativity, Culture and Education*[2], was published in May 1999. It argued for a national strategy for creative and cultural education comparable with the literacy and Numeracy Strategies.

All Our Futures: Creativity, Culture and Education

Our writing of *All Our Futures* drew on evidence from over 300 organisations including subject associations, teacher unions, sectoral organisations for primary, secondary and tertiary education, unions and employers' organisations. We commissioned surveys from the National Foundation for Educational Research on current provision for creative and cultural education within and as a result of the National Curriculum. We convened a series of fifteen special consultative meetings on specialist issues, including design education, dance, drama, science education and others. *All Our Futures* includes details of the results of all of this activity and includes vignettes of provision in each of the main subject areas of the National Curriculum. Overall, the report confirms the anxieties that led to the inquiry being requested in the first place.

The school curriculum and assessment
The National Curriculum has institutionalised a hierarchy of subjects. In every way the 'core' subjects, English, mathematics and science, are seen as more important than the foundation subjects. This is because they have been assumed to be more relevant to the employment prospects of young people and to the economic development of the country as a whole. This view seemed to be confirmed when, in January 1998, the Secretary of State supported by the Chief Inspector of Schools allowed primary schools to relax the teaching of the arts and humanities so that they could concentrate on reaching the national targets for literacy and numeracy. Many of those who contributed to our consultations, especially teachers and head teachers, reported that provision for the arts and humanities in particular, and for creative work in the core subjects too, had been reduced and jeopardised by these measures.

There are problems for creative and cultural education in the restricted range of the school curriculum. But issues of creativity and of cultural development are influenced by more than the formal school curriculum. These influences include methods of teaching the

ethos of schools, and the national priorities that underpin the education service. In particular, they include the methods, styles and criteria of pupil assessment and of school inspection. These are now often inimical to creative work in schools.

Teaching and training
Creative learning is made possible by creative teaching. This is not an easy process and calls for sophisticated skills in teachers. Many teachers feel that their own room for initiative in planning and providing for creative learning are restricted by the high levels of prescription in the National Curriculum and by the overall atmosphere of target setting and of particular styles of public accountability. These constraints are carried through into teacher education. The national standards for teacher education pay little attention to issues of creative and cultural development: the emphasis is on a limited conception of the core subjects. There is no requirement now for any substantive study by trainee teachers of arts and humanities, and effective disincentives to teacher education institutions providing specialist courses in these areas. The result is that over the past ten years, and with increasing speed, colleges and university departments have been closing arts and humanities programmes and departments. There are no now specialist four-year programmes for primary school teachers in the arts. This is a wholly new situation in modern times.

What's the problem?
Why is this? Why do governments say they want to promote creativity in education and then seemingly set about doing the opposite? I think the problem lies in deep-seated misconceptions, and consequent anxieties, about the nature of creativity. These result in, and

are compounded by, a political timidity in tackling the agenda that a real commitment to creativity and human resources require. The persistent mantra of educational policy is the need to raise standards, especially in literacy and numeracy. I am strongly for this and can think of no sensible argument against it. The problem for creativity is that many people associate it in a worried way with 'progressive education'. It is because of the assumed failings of progressive education that standards are thought to have fallen in the first place. For a dozen years, the political remedy has been greater central prescription, a curb on risk taking and an emphasis on quantifiable outcomes and quantitative assessment. And so politicians advocate creativity, but seem to see it in conflict with the standards agenda.

Defining terms

There is a widespread misunderstanding of what creativity is, of how it flourishes or dies. Too often it is associated with laissez faire and being wacky. Or it is thought to be something only certain people have and that cannot therefore be taught. All of this is wrong. On the other hand, there is a desperately narrow view of what standards are in education and of the dynamics of raising them. Too often raising standards is confused with standardisation. This too is a mistake. In *All Our Futures*, we say in detail what we mean by creativity and by culture and we set out the various ways in which they are dynamically related to each other and to raising standards more generally.

In general terms, by creative education we mean forms of education that develop young people's capacities for original ideas and action. By cultural education we mean forms of education that enable them to engage positively with the growing complexity and diversity of social values and ways of life. Creativity is possible in all areas of human activity, including the arts, sciences, at work, at play and in all other areas of daily life. All people have creative abilities and we all have them differently. When individuals find their creative strengths, it can have an enormous impact on self-esteem and on overall achievement. Creativity is not simply a matter of letting go. Serious creative achievement relies on knowledge, control of materials and command of ideas. Creative education involves a balance between teaching knowledge and skills, and encouraging innovation. In these ways, creative development is directly related to cultural education. Young people are living in times of rapid cultural change and diversity. Education must help them to understand different cultural values and traditions and the processes of change and development.

The way ahead

All Our Futures argues for a new balance in education: in setting national priorities; in the structure and organisation of the school curriculum; in methods of teaching and assessment; in relationships between schools and other agencies. It defines creative and cultural education and presents 59 detailed recommendations as a framework for a national strategy. These recommendations address three principal objectives.

Objective One: The School Curriculum and Assessment

To ensure that the importance of creative and cultural education is explicitly recognised and provided for in schools' policies for the whole curriculum, and in Government policy for the National Curriculum.

Objective Two: Teaching and Training

To ensure that teachers and other profes- sionals are encouraged and trained to use methods and materials that facilitate the development of young people's creative abilities and cultural understanding.

Objective Three: Partnerships

To promote the development of the part- nerships between schools and outside agencies that are now essential to provide the kinds of creative and cultural education that young people need and deserve.

Some of these recommendations call for Government action at various levels. But education concerns everybody: children and young people, parents, employers, those in work, out of work or in retire- ment. Consequently, *All Our Futures* is also written for:

- parents, who want education to offer the best opportunities for their children;
- teachers and head teachers who see the potential range and vitality of young people's abilities;
- school governors, who want their schools to be alive with energy and achievement;
- other organisations who see themselves as partners in the education of young people and who want to find better ways of engaging with them; and
- business and union leaders who recognise the need for new approaches to preparing young people for the changing nature of work.

Our aim is to urge the need for a national strategy which engages the energies of all of these to provide the kind of education, in substance and in style, that all young people now need, and to enable them to face an uncertain and demanding future.

The response

All Our Futures has had a huge response from teachers, industry, and from national professional and subject associations. The professional response has been overwhelm- ingly positive and enthusiastic. In the three months following its publication, we hosted meetings with over 70 national organisa- tions, all of which strongly endorsed our arguments and recommendations. The major teacher unions have given the report their full support. So have national associations in the arts, sciences, sport, religion, the human- ities, multicultural education, in business, in special needs and in teacher education. They and many others are keen that as many people as possible should consider the implications of *All Our Futures* for their own work in education and in economic, social and cultural development. The Government has issued a formal response to *All Our Futures* and has begun to act on its recom- mendations. But there is much more to be done.

From policy to practice

During the last twenty years, there have been huge changes in the systems and struc- tures of education. In the past three years there have been numerous initiatives and strategies. But there has been very little debate about fundamental principles, about what we are educating young people for. Instead, successive Governments have doggedly emphasised the need to raise standards. But which standards and why? Over a number of years, the balance of education has been lost. The 'national debate' on education has been expressed as a series of dichotomies: as a choice between the arts or the sciences; the core curriculum or the broad curriculum; between academic standards or creativity; freedom or authority in teaching methods. These dichotomies are unhelpful. Realising the potential of young people, and raising standards of achievement and motivation includes all of these. Creating the right synergy in education is an urgent and complex task, from national policy making to classroom teaching. Many high-performing teachers and schools are already doing what we are recommending. We want to establish national priorities for creative and cultural education in all schools.

In his introduction to *Excellence in Schools*[3], David Blunkett identifies five priorities for education:

- the need to overcome economic and social disadvantages;
- the creation of greater fairness within the education system;
- the encouragement of aspiration;
- economic competitiveness; and
- unlocking the potential of each individual.

These are the right priorities and that they are related. *All Our Futures* aims:

- to show how these priorities can be realised through a systematic approach to creative and cultural education;
- to promote higher standards in creative and cultural education in all disciplines;
- to promote parity of provision between the arts, humanities, sciences and other major areas of education; and
- to stimulate a broad base of partnerships between schools and outside agencies.

Education faces challenges that are without precedent. Meeting these challenges calls for new priorities in education, including a much stronger emphasis on creative and cultural education and a new balance in teaching and in the curriculum.

Conclusion

According to UNESCO, in the next thirty years more people will be gaining formal qualifications through education and training than since the beginning of history. This massive growth in education is fuelled by the impact of new technologies, by the growing need for intellectual labour and by population growth. We cannot meet these extraordinary future challenges just by doing better and more of what we did in the past. We have to do something different. The foundations of the present education system were laid at the end of the nineteenth century. They were designed to meet the needs of a world that was being transformed by industrialisation. The challenges we face now are of the same magnitude, but they are of a different character. The task is not to do better now what we set out to do then: it is to rethink the purposes, methods and scale of education in our new circumstances. *All Our Futures* argues that no education system can be world-class without valuing and integrating creativity in teaching and learning, in the curriculum, in management and leadership and without linking this to understanding cultural change and diversity. This is not an option: it is a necessity.

---

[1] *Excellence in Schools*, DfEE, 1997

[2] *All our Futures: Culture and Education*, the report of the National Advisory Committee on Creative and Cultural Education, DfEE, 1999

[3] *Excellence in Schools*, DfEE, 1997

Goodbye to schools and hello to the neighbourhood learning campus

Phil Street

FROM THE EARLIEST TIMES, SCHOOLS HAVE been places for children and out of bounds to adults, other than a small select band engaged in the process of teaching children. The architecture of older schools suggested they were forbidden territory for anyone other than children. High walls and heavy doors indicated the need to keep the children in and adult influence out. Windows were there for letting in light, not for seeing the outside world through.

The message of limited access was reinforced by formality of behaviour alien to most children and their families and unfamiliar procedures accompanied by an unwritten code of behaviour only decipherable by those brought up in the ways of academia.

Social distance was maintained between school and families. Teachers were invested with authority and were addressed with deference. School teachers were regarded as intellectual superiors removed from the daily humdrum, being members of the scholarly elite.

The education of children was to be vested in the alumni of the ivory towers. Children were to be placed in their care and cloistered away. Schools removed children from the influences and distraction of every day life. Education was to take place in a socially sanitised location free from outside interference and without any impediment that family or neighbours could create.

For some adults their experience of school was just too much. There was little need for high walls and heavy doors to keep them out, recollections of school days were enough to prevent any attempt to return. The clanking of the school gates behind them for the very last time brought a feeling of liberation rather than loss.

The evolution of community schools

Given this model of generational segregation the wonder is that the idea of making schools accessible to the adult community ever came to be considered. The magnitude of Henry Morris's village college idea is difficult to imagine now, but in the 1920s the suggestion of using schools as focal points for community life must have sounded bizarre, if not bordering on insanity.

The sense of relief felt by many on leaving school and the fact that many teachers perceived remoteness as virtuous meant that schools were not the most popular of locations for education for the wider community. Exclusiveness was the symbol of quality and the Board schools of the early twentieth century sought to ape their public school 'betters'.

Despite all this, Morris did persuade the elected members of Cambridgeshire to open schools to the inhabitants of the villages and forward thinkers were found to lead these revolutionary institutions. At around the same time, schools were also being opened in cities and towns in various parts of the country to accommodate evening institutes. These provided evening classes for adults wanting to improve themselves. Amongst the major sources of inspiration for the evening institutes were the nineteenth century mechanics institutes and the early twentieth century Workers Education Association.

The practice formulated in Cambridgeshire by Morris and the introduction of evening institutes formed the high water mark of use of schools by the wider community for some thirty years. It was not until the late forties that Stewart Mason, a disciple of Morris's, began to introduce community colleges in Leicestershire. It was a further twenty years before Robert Aitkin and Robert Nixon, inspired by the work of Eric Midwinter's education priority areas pioneered the urban community schools in Coventry and Walsall.

By the late sixties the term evening institute had been replaced by adult education centre, although the former name stubbornly continued to remain part of common parlance. Adult education centres proliferated, particularly in the big cities. London had a massive programme of adult education, much of it delivered in schools outside the school day. However, although schools were largely the venue for adult education, there was little contact between school management and staff and the employees of the adult education service.

There were a few schools whose interpretation of being a community school had led them to assume responsibility for adult education, but for the most part even those schools that were designated as community schools were, in practice, sophisticated forms of dual use.

By the eighties the combination of new financial management arrangements and education reform had virtually done for community schools and was having an corrosive effect on adult education. The devotees of community education in schools managed to cling on and despite everything, continued to champion wider community involvement, including a programme of adult education.

The legislation of the early nineties led to a major revision of further education, involving its artificial separation into vocational and non-vocational types. This inflicted more damage on community schools and did little for adult education other than reducing its presence still further on school sites.

However, changes in the external environment were not the only factors to impact on the relationship between schools and adult education. A fair percentage of teachers took a traditional view of the school. They saw schools as places for children and young people and felt that the education of adults needed to be pursued elsewhere and by others. A significant number of adult educators were not well disposed towards schools. Many thought adult education was repairing the damage schools had inflicted on adults as children and that any involvement with schools would be largely counter-productive. At the same time there were those amongst teachers and adult educators that saw huge advantages to be gained from close co-operation between schools and adult education. They advocated far closer collaboration and championed initiatives such as parental involvement, adults learning alongside pupils and joint management of adult education programmes.

The current agenda

The past few years have witnessed a new turn of events. Issues of quality, participation, attainment and social inclusion have combined to lead schools and adult educators to reflect more critically on their performance. There has been a growing awareness amongst some teachers that encouraging parental involvement can lead to a direct influence on children's educational achievements. Similarly there is a gradual dawning of the need to involve the community in delivering the curriculum and in reinforcing what children learn in the classroom. Amongst those involved in adult education there has been a wider recognition that new approaches have to be developed to encourage certain parts of the community to return to learn. Adult educators have realised that much of their current client group have already enjoyed a significant amount of education. There is a growing awareness that for adult education to fulfil its potential of being an important player in promoting social inclusion it has to strengthen its links with schools.

This new consciousness means that the enmity that once existed between some in adult education and some teachers has

diminished. Although there are those who still see their roles in separate silos, one occupied by adults and another by children, there is emerging an increasing number who are making the connections between what happens in school and what occurs beyond.

Much needs to be done if this feeling of mutuality is to make meaningful progress. The accusation made by some adult educators that school teachers cannot teach adults has certain validity. Similarly, teachers who emphasise that they entered the profession to exclusively teach children are also right. The initial preparation that teachers and adult educators receive is for the reality they are to enter. This accounts for the fact that few, if any school teachers are trained to work with parents as co-educators or as educators of adults and why those employed in adult education are not equipped to teach pupils in the classroom, nor versed in school organisational culture.

For the differences to be fully overcome we will need to continue to train educators to specialise in one branch of education, but we need to encourage them to share some common experiences and develop an appreciation of one another's work.

However, training in itself will not be enough. Approaches to leadership and management will have to alter. Headteachers or principals may have to consider that they do not lead the type of schools with which we are accustomed. In future schools will be learning campuses. It needs to be, good-bye to schools and hello to neighbourhood learning campuses. This will equally apply to primary as well as secondary schools. Experience suggests that adults, and especially parents, find accessing a primary school a good deal easier than secondary schools. Primary schools are the place where children first enter the education system, perhaps primary schools could assume a gateway function for adults and this could be a first point of re-entry. Certainly family education and parental involvement projects of the kind operated by Community Education Development Centre (CEDC) such as SHARE, have demonstrated the capacity to attract adults back into learning who would not have used any other routes.

Leadership and management will play a key role in promoting adult learning through schools. It has been proved over and over again that leadership is crucial to organisational culture and purpose. The success, or otherwise, of a school active in its community is heavily influenced by the attitude and importance given to it by the headteacher. Work with adults has to be valued right at the very top of a school if it is to be taken seriously. These leaders have to acknowledge that the conditions and the approaches to work with adults are necessarily different to those required for teaching pupils.

However, the influence of leaders will only stretch so far. Those following will also have to be convinced. The tradition of schools as places only for children has a long pedigree. Classroom teachers have to recognise the value of activities with adults to their work. Currently the case for this is being made at various levels, but the arguments have to be constantly reinforced. Likewise, those involved in adult education will need to be convinced that an intense working relationship with schools will advance their purpose.

The effect of parental involvement on pupils' learning is widely understood and well documented, but perhaps less widely recognised is the effect adults can have on young people as lifelong learning role models. The specific gains that can be made from drawing upon the community to enrich or even deliver the curriculum continues to influence only a few teachers and the term the community-active National Curriculum enjoyed only a brief airing.

Future provision of learning opportunities for adults in schools will only partly be accounted for in terms understood in the past. Schools have to remain a venue for adult education organised by others, but a more integrated approach to work with adults needs to be fostered. Contrary to the opinion held by some, adult influence can be a force for the good. Exposure to the wider community can prepare young people for adult life, can reinforce learning in the classroom and can encourage young minds to recognise the importance of being lifelong learners.

Presently, the inspection system of schools exerts enormous influence on what schools regard as important. Whatever earns approbation from school inspectors is pursued with vigour. A schools inspection report has a fundamental effect on its fortunes. Consequently, any activities pursued by the school that do not attract the inspector's attention will be afforded limited significance. This would suggest that the value schools attach to providing learning opportunities for adults would be substantially advanced if it were to figure in the inspection procedure.

Resources are also an impediment to promoting adult learning opportunities in schools. The current funding arrangements make it difficult for schools to access finance to enable adult learning. Further education funding goes either directly to colleges or through sponsorship to Local Education Authorities. Local authorities also receive the money for non-vocational adult education. Consequently, schools have to go through a time consuming procedure to have any chance of accessing funds.

The Learning and Skills Councils offer the opportunity to change that and make it possible for schools to obtain direct access to funding. By allowing schools to make applications to the Learning and Skills Council a message would be going out to schools legitimising their role in providing learning opportunities for adults.

Perhaps the issue that may have the most potent effect on drawing schools and adult educators together could be social inclusion. Most of us recognise that a propensity to learn has an important effect on our life chances. Yet we also know that levels of participation in learning remain modest. Learning is central to addressing social inclusion. Amongst the barriers to participation are distance, anxiety about entering learning institutions and discomfort about being unsuccessful.

People in deprived communities do not commute to learn, they find certain institutions intimidating and do not want any sense of low self-esteem further reinforced. It is arguable that the close location of schools and the fact that they are familiar, if not always welcoming, suggests they have the potential to play an important role in the future education of adults.

However, physical buildings are not enough in themselves. There is a need for appropriate advice, teaching skills and support structures. Surely this is where the professionalism of adult educators is critical. Perhaps a key aspect of the neighbourhood learning campuses is advice and guidance for adult learners and opportunities tutored and supported by those trained and competent to work with adults. Maybe the advanced skills teacher of the future will be capable of both leading a Year 5 class or a group of adult learners.

Ironically, there seems to be an enormous adult education programme to be undertaken with education management, teachers and adult educators if schools are to break once and for all with the image of being a place where children are cloistered away and adults are present only under sufferance.

There are already examples of schools where the presence of adults is seen as natural and beneficial. The number of these schools is growing, but slowly. If the experience of the past one hundred and thirty years of schooling in this country is to be challenged attitudes and values have to change. Schools cannot continue to be examples of generational apartheid. We need public schools that are public places. We also need to welcome the neighbourhood campus.

The school of the future: a view from the Secondary Heads Association

Tony Hinkley

THINK BACK TO THE CAR YOU WERE DRIVING in 1975. How does it compare with your present car? Nostalgia aside, there is little doubt that you had not dreamt that a typical family car would have air conditioning, electric windows, power assisted steering, ABS, and so on. What about schools? How are they different from today? Spirit duplicators, 16mm projectors, chalk and the cane compared with computers, video projectors, interactive white boards and counselling!

Now, imagine Britain in twenty five years time. Will we see the science fiction version of transport, teleportation, or simply faster, safer, more comfortable and economically friendly cars than we now know? And education in 2025? More of the same with technological knobs on? Or is there a chance that we might not only see radical change, but actually take the bull by the horns and bring it about?

Consider also the widely held view that schools are designed for a time and a purpose that no longer exist. What does it mean in reality and what are the issues for schools?

It is becoming as easy to communicate and trade with a country on the other side of the world as with a neighbour. The world has become smaller than ever and peoples' expectations across the world have changed. Newspapers, television and radio are broadcast on the Internet; shopping catalogues are accessible to everyone in the world with a computer; educational materials and opportunities are available as never before. In this context, therefore, education needs, and is likely, to undergo transformational change. Already, year-on-year, there are changes occurring that would have been unthinkable in the recent past. But a school of the future is not simply a school of the present with more ICT kit.

The Secondary Heads Association (SHA) recognises the need for an evolutionary approach to change so as to enable educators and the public, both typically conservative in their view of education, to accommodate the culture change involved. In evolution, of course, some things will die. Accepting and coping with this is part of the challenge. This chapter seeks to explore some of the questions around this area and offers a glimpse at some of the sorts of answers we may produce.

Central direction, support and, perhaps most importantly, vision will be needed to unify the nation in a common set of purposes and methodologies for education. Certainly there will be a need to challenge the forces of conservatism among the profession and the public alike. Generally people do not mind change, but they do not like being changed. We must carry the profession and others with us in this.

Future provision – learning centres and communities of learners?

Imagine this: learning activities based on Community Learning Centres with video-conferencing and e-mail linking learners, leaders and administrators. Homes would also be linked to the Learning Centres electronically, as would employers and higher and further education. Is this not already a reality in some parts of the country and, if so, then what might we imagine in 25 years time? Indeed, is it even imaginable with any sense of reality?

Would we recognise teachers as we do now, or would classrooms themselves be rather different in organisation and activity? Perhaps a classroom might be a resource base, where students of all ages drop in for academic support sessions as we might do now at a health clinic. This would certainly have implications for the training of staff before and during service.

A wide range of courses and opportunities, academic, vocational and occupational, might be offered, physically and electronically. Familiar patterns of the school day and year, and the nature of 'a day in school' would change – but how? The concept of a term would have to change as learning becomes related to personal targets. This might alleviate the current debate about the three-, four- or five-term year.

Obviously, curriculum experience would be as varied as appropriate, and a minimum core would need to be agreed. We have to ask how this would meet future needs that we cannot yet even imagine. Approaches to assessment will need to diagnose learning needs and to demonstrate competence or attainment. There is already much agreement that the timing of assessment should be 'when ready' rather than at certain ages. How this would manifest itself as currency for employment or education is yet to be defined.

Community Learning Centres must surely see themselves a leaders of the educational and learning processes, taking the initiative in such areas as the development of family learning opportunities (more than simply learning 'schoolwork' in the family). Education must be inclusive for all.

Funding for the centres will be up for debate. Will Community Learning Centres be funded from private and public sources, for example? Other important issues include governance regulations; integration with existing national and local policy; national conditions of service for teachers (including school and college leaders) and national and local priorities. If education is a 'whole life' process, the challenge will be how we capture and recognise learning that takes place elsewhere other than at the Community Learning Centres. Indeed, the fundamental conceptual issues around the need for such places as Community Learning Centres also remains to be challenged.

Approaches to learning

The main role of Community Learning Centres in the future would be to develop in young people the skills and attitudes that will enhance their natural state as learners. If learning is defined as a change in state of the individual (for example in terms of skill, knowledge, attitude or behaviour), then the importance of interaction between individuals must be recognised. So how will these learning centres, with their drop-in facility, be able to co-ordinate these possibly conflicting demands?

Who would argue with the concept of a Learning Society, where learning is valued, encouraged and facilitated for all? This concept remains a cliché unless strategies are in place to deliver the vision. The question here is how to achieve this ideal. What might be the role of Community Learning Centres in the teaching of parenting skills? In this area we have, perhaps, only just begun to scratch the surface of understanding the connections between diet, health, environment and the capacity to learn.

How might the developing understanding of how we learn inform future provision? A portfolio of achievement might become the norm rather than a set of examination results. Or would this undermine the 'gold standard' which is held precious by some (as though there is a standard which does not vary over time)?

Students of all ages will need to understand and use the potential of their brain. The emphasis is rightly moving from teaching to learning. Again, we need to investigate what motivates people to learn and identify and remove the barriers to learning and motivation. An increased awareness of the importance of the emotional state of the learner is vital. The concept of 'high challenge – low threat' as the most productive learning environment must be embedded in learning situations and programmes.

Will encouraging children at a certain age to have more experience of the world of work, including paid employment, lead to better motivation of the learner and greater involvement from the community? This is an area of potential for the development of some of the social and team skills that are valued.

Social roles of learning centres

We must make sure we fill the 'moral vacuum'. It will be important not to overlook the social, moral and ethical contribution schools do, and will continue to, make to society. Currently many schools provide the 'social glue' giving structure and certainties to many young people and their families, whereas life is often lacking such structure and is full of uncertainties. There is an increasing sense in which schools and, by definition teachers, are taking on these complex roles, and a sense of the expectations on schools and teachers becoming untenable unless something changes.

One approach may be for the Community Learning Centre to be part of what is, in effect, a multi-agency approach, as many Education Action Zones are attempting to achieve. What would be the implications here for the tutorial function in schools and personal, social and health education, and citizenship? Should it be the role of Community Learning Centres to promote debate about such issues and to encourage understanding and tolerance, or should learning centres focus on academic attainment only?

There is currently a clear tension between the roles of schools as experts in curriculum pedagogy and the social roles schools have to play (both implicitly and explicitly). Can Community Learning Centres be non-judgemental or ideologically free since they are necessarily founded in a socio-economic base, carrying with them as they will their own social, political and economic baggage? We must continue the debate as to who is to define the social and political context in which Community Learning Centres are to operate.

Overall, Community Learning Centres will have to be proactive in providing each student with the life skills to cope and to thrive in a complex and culturally diverse society. Part of the social and educational role of Community Learning Centres will involve the development of the autonomous individual. Therefore they will have to consider how to provide learners with more power to make choices about the content, form and direction of their own learning. This is a challenge not to be taken lightly. It will require courage and courageous leadership.

Leadership roles

Vision is a key aspect of leadership, and school leaders must continue to provide the inspiration for others to achieve what they might not have imagined possible. As well as leading learning, we must be the leading learners in our organisations and communities and set the necessary personal example to others.

There will be leadership requirements for head teachers (what name will replace this outdated description?) for setting and maintaining moral and ethical stances and maintaining an appropriate ethos. Leaders and leadership teams will, therefore, continue to require co-ordination skills and maintenance of a cohesive overall view. The ability to have a 'presence' for students and staff in such diverse arrangements as described will require advanced skills of

communication, including a facility for using developing technologies.

Given that, how will we ensure our new leaders are adequately prepared for this role, and how will the selection procedure remove the vagaries of a selection process controlled by lay people with no accountability as at present? Similarly, the development of the role of the leadership team and its organisation, recruitment and training will be vital.

Will teachers lose their responsibility for curriculum pedagogy and merely follow central dictat? They will certainly need to develop further their professional expertise in the newer areas of leading learning, rather than the management of teaching. Development of assessment strategies that are competence based and the management of groups that are not necessarily age related provide other examples of the changes and challenges. How will teachers be prepared for these new approaches?

Teacher workload increasingly is becoming recognised as a problem and the issue of 'teacher as parent-substitute' as opposed to 'teacher as learning director' must become resolved. There may be different specialists for different roles, and these specialists may not always be teachers. Either way there will be a need for flexibility due to the diversity of opportunity provided by the education system, and the likely inclusion of more classroom assistants for students of all ages.

The role of the governors in ensuring that the system works is likely to be enhanced. The role of Ofsted and auditors is also likely to change and maybe increase. The functions of a local authority seem likely to diminish as the various kinds of expertise they used to provide become embodied in the school and the inspectorial and statistical functions go to Ofsted.

Community Learning Centres that are completely porous, in other words, which operate as twenty-four hour, 365 day-a-year schools, will require different management. What will be the approach to governance in order to fulfil this different role in the community? Schools must become more community focussed and communities must become more involved in the support of their schools, but what will this mean in reality?

At SHA, we are determined to prepare for a time we shall not see. We welcome comment and support in our mission to change the face of education. We believe that the time is ripe to persuade government and the nation that we must agree a new set of principles, plan for the changes needed and act to create the education system our children deserve.

Finally, party political influence should be minimised whilst achieving national political support. Education must become a national cause not a political football. This may yet prove to be the greatest challenge of all.

Schools and employability: new roles for teachers

Ann Evans

D RIVEN LARGELY BY RAPIDLY DEVELOPING
technological change and globalisation, work is vastly different today
compared to twenty years ago. As the RSA
has put it, "Work is redefining itself".[1]

This chapter seeks to understand the implications of changes in the workplace for
schools now and in the future.

> "At the centre of this transformation lies the
> progression from the industrial society, based
> at its heart upon the physical capital of land,
> plant and raw materials, to an information
> and knowledge based society, built upon the
> intellectual capital, the knowledge, imagina-
> tion and creativity of our people." [2]
> Chris Humphries, CBE, Director General,
> British Chambers of Commerce

It is generally accepted that there is no
longer a job for life. Short-term contracts
that demand highly skilled resources to
complete discreet parcels of work give
organisations flexibility and competitive
advantage. Electronic communication means
that these skilled workers can be recruited
from literally anywhere in the world.
Workplaces can even be located far from
the point of sale, where workers with the
right attributes and competencies can be
found. HSBC spends nearly two billion dol-
lars on information technology each year.
They choose to have four main systems

development sites: in Hong Kong, Canada,
the USA and the UK. But potentially they
could be anywhere.

Technologies, such as e-commerce conducted over the Internet, enable business to
become internationally mobile in a way
never possible before. Newly appointed
headteachers, equipped with their laptops,
are also experiencing a lack of boundaries in
online conferencing about leadership issues.
Schools are beginning to link with other
schools inside and beyond the UK via video-
conference and the Internet. When this
increasingly becomes the norm, there will
be a whole new set of implications for
educational buildings and resources.

Global competition has intensified to
unprecedented levels, stimulating business
re-engineering often through the use of
the Internet. For example, Microsoft
claims to save $3 million a year by using
an Internet-based procurement system.
Airlines purportedly save up to 75% of
processing costs through online ticket
sales. Walmart spends millions on integrating its systems with those of suppliers
to finely control stock levels. Even smaller
companies supplying large organisations
are being asked to use supply chain
systems. Companies can pay a heavy price
for failing to respond to such calls to
change business methods.

Virtual organisations reduce the need for expensive office space. Business functions such as technical support and the distribution of information and resources via Internet technology can take place independently of geographical location, time zones and high reproduction and storage costs. What implications will this have for how we purchase items for schools?

The re-engineering of business requires talented, skilled, innovative, creative and entrepreneurial individuals. This is a major issue that the curriculum must take on board with utmost urgency. Pupils in schools will require these essential skills for the future workplace in addition to their core subjects. Other qualities and skills necessary in today's workplace were identified by Heads, Teachers and Industry's (HTI's) Strategic Partnership Forum, a collaborative think tank of senior business executives:

"A flexible response to change, willingness to take risks, lateral thinking, having resilience and the will, being able to take charge, be autonomous...This is what we need. And having intellectual wisdom, too – skills of analysis and the ability to handle data...People have to collaborate and work together".[3]

The need for lifelong learners

The pace of change and demands of the workplace today require a love of learning and the motivation to continue learning throughout life. Sir Nicholas Goodison, Deputy Chairman of Lloyds TSB Group plc and Honorary President of HTI Leadership and Management, a national educational charity, summarised the reasons why lifelong learning is key to the success of individuals, business and the nation. He said:

"Lifelong learning is not a luxury. It is an essential. It is essential for at least three reasons: first, there are seven million adults in the UK who have no qualifications. Eight million have serious difficulties with numeracy and literacy. These are terrible figures. Second, those who are qualified face a future of constant revolution – revolution in knowledge, technology, communications, markets, risk, organisational structures and politics. They need to hone their skills, broaden their knowledge and prepare themselves for change if they are to succeed, and if they are to seize opportunities when they change jobs, which is far more likely today than in the past.
Third, we are a trading nation relying on the skills of our people to ensure that we can compete successfully in the world marketplace. In November 1998, the Chancellor underlined the point: "...to meet the productivity challenge, we must do far more to encourage the ambitions of all our children, not least by bringing the world of education and the world of work into closer contact".[4]

How can young people be prepared for the challenges of the modern workplace? Education has a fundamental role to play in developing and channelling the diverse abilities of all young people into the skills and knowledge required by tomorrow's businesses. This has profound implications for education and business.

Changing the curriculum

It is not the intention of this article to dwell on the need to modernise the curriculum and education system, whose origins and legacy lie in the nineteenth century. However, the Royal Society of Arts proposals, contained in *Opening Minds* published in 1999, to develop a curriculum based on competencies, rather than acquisition of knowledge, is to be welcomed.[5] The report contends that there are five broad categories each with a number of individual competencies which students need to develop in order to function successfully as adults. They are:

Competencies for learning, e.g. understand how to learn, taking account of their preferred learning styles, and understand the need to, and how to, manage their own learning throughout life;
Competencies for citizenship, e.g. understand how society, government and business work and the importance of active citizenship;
Competencies for relating to people, e.g. understand how to operate in teams, and their own capacities for filling different team roles;
Competencies for managing situations, e.g. understand what is meant by managing change, and have developed a range of techniques for use in varying situations; and
Competencies for managing information, e.g. understand the importance of reflecting and applying critical judgement, and have learned how to do so.

The RSA Curriculum relies on subject content as the medium through which these competencies can be developed, with assessment based on competencies achieved rather than the acquisition of knowledge. Calls by Chris Humphries and Ken Robinson, Professor of Creative Education University of Warwick, for the development of entrepreneurial and creative skills within a re-engineered curriculum are also to be greeted enthusiastically.

Closer links with business
Equally critical to the development of the competencies necessary for the employee of the future is the imperative for closer links between business and education. However, these links should come under the umbrella of a coherent national strategy. A national strategy for education business links, which are vital to the creation of a successful Britain, is long overdue. Everyone agrees that more should be done to encourage them and to concentrate activities on the real needs of young people, schools and business. There are many examples of productive partnerships between education and business, but they have tended to be ad hoc, largely driven by major corporates and, while successful on their own merits, not galvanised by a clearly defined nationals strategy. National strategy is the responsibility of the Government but, once in place, the demands of a rapidly changing workplace, a re-engineered curriculum and closer education business links would have profound and challenging implications for the role of teachers.

Rooted in an environment which has not fundamentally changed since the industrial nineteenth century and, in most cases, never having experienced working life outside education, there is an urgent need for teachers to undertake secondments in business as part of their professional development. This will enable them to become aware of the rapidly changing workplace. This has been recognised by the Government in its proposals for the National College for School Leadership. However, HTI has understood the benefits of attaching teachers to businesses for a long time. Founded in 1986, it aims to enhance educational leadership and management in the UK. HTI arranges secondments for senior educationalists into business as managers.

To prepare young people for a rapidly changing world, school leaders will need to become deeply aware of employability issues. HTI's leadership secondment programme provides the opportunity for senior educationalists to become immersed in a business culture for periods of up to a year. It is this immersion in a different culture which gives them a profound, and personal, understanding of business needs. The experience of doing a real managerial job in industry gives them a first hand understanding of the world awaiting their pupils.

Leaving their comfort zones to enter an unfamiliar business world, HTI secondees become risk-takers. They gain confidence by succeeding in an unfamiliar environment. They return to education refreshed and revitalised with a willingness to give their pupils the space to take risks and responsibility for their own learning. They have a deeper understanding of the competencies which organisations require of their students. They also develop their skills in leadership, management, marketing, staff development and customer care.

A reshaped curriculum in which assessment is based on the development of competencies, rather than the acquisition of knowledge, would totally change the nature of teaching. Of course, the need for fundamental literacy and numeracy skills will never change. Beyond this, teachers would no longer be the founts of all knowledge, but would act as facilitators, guiding students to how and where they can access the required information. Acting as coaches, they would seek to develop students'

initiative, analytical and thinking powers. Learning activities would be designed to foster team working, collaboration, lateral thinking and a love of learning and discovery. Undoubtedly, the skills that effective teachers display under the current circumstances would be increasingly valuable e.g. good communication and organisational skills, leadership and management qualities and multi-tasking. However, ICT skills would be essential in order to take advantage of all the electronic learning opportunities available and drive through the possibilities of virtual schools.

In order to foster closer links with business, teachers would need to develop as relationship managers, to sustain meaningful associations with key business partners in which they are able to identify entrepreneurial opportunities for enhancing the quality of educational output.

Acquiring all these additional skills for the school of the future calls for careful recruitment and selection of teachers and a radical approach to teacher training.

The role of teachers will be crucial to the success in the twenty first century, a point endorsed recently by David Puttnam, the new Chairman of the General Teaching Council, when he said, "A successful Britain is built on the generation of highly trained, highly skilled and brilliantly motivated teachers".[6]

[1] Valerie Bayliss, *Redefining Work*, RSA 1998

[2] HTI Leadership and Management and Education and Youth Ltd, 'Executive Forum: Today's leaders – Tomorrow's world, Developing a national strategy for business to work with education', Conference Report, 2000

[3] Margaret Wilkins, *Are the 3 Rs enough?*, HTI Issues Paper 1 1997

[4] Sir Nicholas Goodison, Deputy Chairman, Lloyds TSB Group plc and Honorary President of HTI Leadership and Management, in Headway 8, HTI, 1999

[5] Valerie Bayliss, *Opening Minds*, RSA, London, 1999

[6] HTI Leadership and Management and Education and Youth Ltd, 'Executive Forum: Today's leaders - Tomorrow's world, Developing a national strategy for business to work with education', Conference Report, 2000

Local Authorities, schools and lifelong learning

Tony Breslin

THE RECENT LANGUAGE OF EDUCATIONAL change has been the language of good ideas: school improvement, raising achievement, education for citizenship, widening participation, Key Skills and lifelong learning. In the language of good ideas, the concepts that hold the language together pre-empt rebuttal by virtue of their inherent goodness. For who could disagree with school improvement, with the development of Key Skills, with widening participation or with lifelong learning? As always, though, the problem with such concepts is one of definition. Key Skills, for example, in various guises and formations have been around since the late 1980s, but are only now approaching a plausible definition with their articulation through the Key Skills Qualification. Under the astute stewardship of Bernard Crick, Education for Citizenship has made swifter progress, but is unlikely to be embedded in the minds of either curriculum planners or students before the middle of the current decade. School improvement, meanwhile, although universally sought, has yet to have a common and shared meaning among students, parents, teachers or academics, such that the minor matter of improvement 'from what' and 'to what' requires clarification and agreement.

Defining lifelong learning

So it is with lifelong learning. Learning is a good thing and that it is lifelong is better still. But, beyond being agreed as a universal good,

little has been done to unpick precisely what is meant by lifelong learning. Thus, in Autumn 1998, when council and education authority advisers and officers began to receive the first of a plethora of papers relating to lifelong learning, there was little to guide them on the precise meaning of the new mantra. In some documents lifelong learning was about compensatory education for adults focused around the development of basic skills, in others it referred to the attempts to bring coherence to the Further Education sector, elsewhere it began with work related learning provision for disaffected 14 year-olds and occasionally, with a degree of greater enlightenment, it was associated with Family Learning, specifically parental numeracy and literacy.

Charged with developing LEA Lifelong Learning Development Plans and forming, with colleagues from other authorities and agencies, sub-regional Lifelong Learning Partnerships, these advisers and officers were faced with a challenging terrain. In particular, this terrain seemed to offer three unhelpful characteristics: an absence of any engagement with the process of learning or the new understandings around this; a focus on lifelong learning as a deficit based compensatory model that presumed earlier educational failure at school; an assumption that lifelong learning followed compulsory schooling, such that it was not 'lifelong' at all but set out from a range of age related starting points that differed between document and funding provider. In short, lifelong learning did not so much lack definition as suffer from a range of competing and contradictory definitions linked only by their compensatory pessimism, their 'unlifelong nature' and their failure to engage with the emerging knowledge about learning itself.[1]

In this chapter I want to argue five points: first, that lifelong learning requires definition if it is to prove to be the educational good that its title suggests; second, that if the emergence of a common culture of lifelong learning is to succeed in heralding a Learning Age for all, it must address the limitations and weaknesses inherent in the conceptual-isations of lifelong learning set out in this early documentation and that it must do so through an objectives based approach; third, that any resultant model of lifelong learning must, indeed, be lifelong and embrace schools as central, both as sites for commu-nity learning and as development centres for lifelong learners, with all the implications for school pedagogy that flow from this; fourth, that local agencies (Local Authorities, LEAs, Education-Business Partnerships, Lifelong Learning Partnerships and Learning and Skills Councils) can play a central role in supporting the development of learning cultures and communities through working with schools, colleges, training providers and the community and voluntary sector as partners in this process; fifth, that local authorities, especially but not exclusively through their LEAs, have a key role in build-ing these cultures and communities and the networks that support them.

An objectives based approach

The definitional crisis of lifelong learning set out above is, of course, hardly surprising: a new educational concept, expressed through the language of good ideas and complete with funding streams in place or promised, one which has a proper place in the work of every education or training provider (or aspirant provider) is let loose on a fragmented, resource hungry practitioner community and a resultant contest for inclusion ensues. In this context, it is hardly surprising that the models of lifelong learning offered by the further education sector, the library service, the work based training community and the voluntary sector should differ, and somewhat inevitable that their early attempts at co-operation through local Lifelong Learning Partnerships should be, as in some areas they have been, more like the last days of a difficult marriage than the first of a brave, if experimental, relationship, especially when each has answered to a different set of vows at the altar.

The challenge is to win the case, on this occasion, for the brave new relationship, to live with its intrinsic untidiness and to make it work. Lifelong learning does not sit within the traditional and reassuringly regularised structure of the school timetable or even the neat levels of the emerging qualifications structure, as important as these devices can be as scaffolds for most learners some of the time. Rather, provision in any locality has to be on a multi-agency and trans-disciplinary basis offering a multitude of entry and departure points so that learners can gain access to blocks of learning and qualifications appro-priate to their needs at particular times. This, though, is not to say that the messiness of the genuine learning community cannot be accompanied by route maps for the learner and supported by a set of shared objectives among providers brought together through local networks and panels convened and facilitated by local authorities and others that have some proximity to a democratic mandate.

Precisely because the objectives of lifelong learning have been assumed to be unquestionably 'good', they have been insufficiently aired or explored. Let us explore what, at a basic level, these might be. This may enable us to tease out the kind of definitional clarity that the lifelong learning project has so far lacked. It should also clarify the role of the school, the local authority and other local agencies in the process.

As a minimum, I want to argue that any approach to lifelong learning might seek to build learning participation and achievement in a particular setting with three objectives in mind:
• to increase personal well being and fulfilment;
• to develop active citizenship and political literacy; and
• to enhance workforce membership and full economic literacy and participation.

The first objective suggests an approach to learning that emphasises leisure, enlightenment and the opportunity for creativity; the second complements this with a concern for empowerment, participation and justice; the third underlines the regenerative potential of learning as a means of securing workforce access, economic progression and wealth creation. Of course, different partners in the provision process might emphasise different objectives, but through participating the learner should be able to access provision that will support any or all of the objectives: numeracy or literacy programmes; job related training to enhance workforce opportunities; community development schemes to build local political understanding; interest led learning to develop a new

talent or a long held aspiration or simply as a first nervous step on the learning ladder. Others may modify these objectives or substitute alternative ones, but the consequence, in terms of provision, of any objectives based approach is that:
• provision is offered in a range of settings, often on a multi-disciplinary and trans-disciplinary basis;
• provision is contextualised within a coherent overall strategy, based on the objectives established, which has a coherence to the learner and the potential learner;
• any overall strategy is characterised by an inclusive and holistic approach; and
• the learner has the capacity, or the means to build the capacity, to participate in learning.

Thus, the challenge for those seeking to build learning cultures and learning communities is to allow a dynamic diversity of provision and providers set within, or at least positioned in relation to, a coherent, objectives based and publicly stated strategy which renders this dynamic diversity coherent and accessible to a learner or potential learner. This learner has the capacity to make the most of any learning opportunity offered because they have been encouraged to develop, following the advocacy of the Campaign for Learning, both an appetite and a capacity for learning. In summary, they have learned to learn and are able to enjoy and gain the full benefit of learning in the process.

A multi-agency, trans-disciplinary and objectives based approach of this type has two further consequences. Firstly, it requires a local planning forum of some form: the local authority, the LEA or an organisation such as a local learning panel, which draws together the main providers and representatives of learners as well as potential learners, so that both the objectives and the provision itself can be clarified and matched to local need and reviewed on a regular basis. Secondly, it implies an approach to 'lifelong' learning that is genuinely lifelong, crossing and transcending the boundaries that define conventional educational phases, involving the youngest child and the oldest adult. As such, this does not leave schools as an optional extra in the lifelong learning project. Rather, it places them at the heart of what the London Borough of Enfield has described as a '0+' approach to lifelong learning, resolving the definitional impasse in so doing. It is to this issue, the role of schools in the Learning Age, that I now turn.

Generating an appetite and capacity for learning in schools

At a time when schools are under particular pressure to deliver improved performance, the suggestion that they have yet another responsibility, not simply to their students but to the wider community that they serve, may seem less than inspired. I want to contest that. Embracing such a responsibility, to be the key learning champions for their communities, can be a means of increasing their effectiveness in reaching the kind of targets already laid down by the standards agenda and all that flows from it.

The rationale for placing schools at the heart of the lifelong learning project is essentially three fold.

Firstly, if one is to embrace a '0+' approach to lifelong learning, schools become strategic staging posts along the lifelong learning journey, preceded by childcare, nursery provision and parent support projects, such as Sure Start, and followed by further and higher education, work based training and

adult and community education. Their strategic importance is that they become the key arenas in which young people become learners for life. Thus, school is a period when learning styles and preferences are identified, a knowledge of the formal learning and qualification structure is developed and provisional future learning pathways are set out. Students learn to learn, they develop a love of learning and, indeed, of particular approaches to learning, they are introduced to the range of future learning opportunities that are likely to be open to them and they embark on certain lifelong learning accreditation frameworks, such as that offered by the emerging Key Skills framework, that will endure and be maintained beyond any formal school leaving age. Whatever, the aim should be, to quote Enfield's Lifelong Learning Development Plan:

"...to develop in younger people an appetite and a capacity for learning that continues to grow after the conclusion of their formal schooling[2]."

Secondly, schools ought to embrace the lifelong learning agenda because of their symbolic and practical significance as neighbourhood learning centres, as Tom Bentley has argued.[3] Here, of course there are other potential sites such as colleges, libraries, youth clubs and family health centres and these should play a role in any and every learning community. However, the school provides a reference point in the learning chronology of every member of the community, albeit chequered in some cases, and reaches every parent through its work with younger people. In this context, the potential of the school to widen the participation of older, often socially excluded, individuals in the learning process is phenomenal, whether this be through employing them as classroom assistants, engaging them in Family Learning classes or school based programmes, involving them in the delivery and support of the extra curricular agenda or evaluating the learning progress of pupils through parents' evenings and the like.

And the pay off for schools and their students for this involvement in the lifelong learning project ought to be obvious: developing students' appetites and capacities as learners and building stronger bridges with parents through parental involvement and Family Learning initiatives can only serve to support the standards and achievement agenda. Through the development of focused lifelong learning strategies, supportive, involved parents and motivated students, so long the bedrock of the successful middle class school of the suburbs, can emerge as key elements in the raising achievement and school improvement programmes of school communities in much more challenging settings.

None of this is easy. Becoming a 'Lifelong Learning School' as Longworth and Davies phrase the challenge, is hard work.[4] It requires a revisioning of how the school operates such that learning to learn and the diagnosis of learning styles and preferences takes on a parity with learning geography or science or French or mathematics and supports this subject based activity. It requires a new focus in initial and continuing teacher education programmes that underlines the importance of learning and a sensitivity to different learners' needs. The recent focus on Thinking Skills and the emergence of Birmingham's University of the First Age initiative, with its focus around the out of school hours agenda, new approaches to learning and the staging of Super Learning Days, may offer conduits for progress here, but there is much work to be done.[5]

It means a new approach to relationships with parents, especially the parents of the under achieving, the excluded and the apparently disaffected. Secondary school parents' evenings, for example, need to become more than simply a set of eight or nine subject based meetings in a crowded impersonal hall, each resulting in another telling off for the parent and their under achieving off-spring alike. Parent-friendly schools are vital if schools are to become important hubs in the learning community, especially for those for whom schools were not child friendly the first time around. Finally, the curriculum and qualification structure needs to evolve away from the current 'one size and style fits all' model that sees, in the average secondary school 200 hundred learners, united only by the rough proximity of their birthdays, sit their English GCSE on the same day. While the new flexibility in Key Stage 4 of the National Curriculum offers some grounds for hope, schools and, more so, the DfEE have much to learn from the modularised models employed in the best work based learning models and, increasingly, in Higher Education.

The need is for a less age-related approach to curricular delivery and the celebration of a broader band of achievement. As the recently retired former Director of the University of London's Institute of Education has remarked "a school system based around failure provides no foundation for lifelong learning" and yet failure is inevitable for a significant number as long as we persist with a one size and style model.[6] Indeed, an irony of the raising achievement agenda is that the greater the progress of the majority, the greater the potential exclusion of those who do not get over the learning barriers that, for this group, examinations are. The greater the pass percentage, the more exposed the failed remainder, the less successful they are likely to be as future learners and the harder the work of the lifelong learning project as something genuinely inclusive and holistic for all.

Herein lies the third reason for placing schools at the heart of the lifelong learning agenda: the contradiction at the core of much current lifelong learning practice is addressed. It is this contradiction that has produced the definitional crisis of the lifelong learning agenda set out in the opening sections of this chapter. Much of the thinking around the conceptualisation of lifelong learning that underpins the current policy focus in this area of educational reform has emerged from the Government's proper concern with social exclusion. As the levels of adult illiteracy and under qualification indicate,[7] "the injustice of the nation's unequal learning record"[8] as Jim Smith and Andrea Spurling put it, as labour market data suggests, as school truancy and exclusion data underlines and as a whole range of social exclusion data emphasises[9], there is clearly a crisis around social exclusion that needs to be addressed now.

However, if the reaction is merely and solely to pump funding into providing compensatory post compulsory education in basic skills for those who have been failed by yesterday's schools, the lifelong learning project as an expression of optimism for a better tomorrow is lost for good. An optimistic model of lifelong learning must combine meeting the needs of today's socially excluded adults, where appropriate utilising schools as sites for their support, with meeting the requirements of tomorrow's successful and committed adults, by developing their potential, appetite and capacity as learners in today's schools. The short term policy fix is in danger of clouding out the long term problems that arise from it: a deficit model of lifelong learning focused only around 'catch up' precludes the possibility of a learning rich future built by learning communities making learning cultures a reality.

Building learning cultures and learning communities:

The plethora of definitions cited earlier for lifelong learning itself is matched only by the range of existing or soon to be formed local agencies that have emerged to take the lifelong learning project forward. Thus, local councils and specific council directorates, Local Education Authorities, government regional offices, Further Education colleges, local Training Enterprise Councils, private training providers, Education Business Partnerships, careers service companies, and various community and voluntary groups have all either laid claim to, or expressed a fairly forceful interest in, the lifelong learning field and, more particularly, its associated funding streams.

True, the formation of Local Lifelong Learning Partnerships and the requirement placed on them to develop Strategic Lifelong Learning Plans, the responsibility of LEAs to produce Borough Lifelong Learning Development Plans supported through an associated channel of the Standards Fund, and the imminent formation of Learning Skills Councils, together with associated reforms in inspection and guidance frameworks, is gradually bringing a degree of coordination, "co-opetition rather than cooperation" as one FE based colleague put it recently.[10] As a route map, though, to personal and community learning opportunities, this A-Z of Lifelong Learning remains one that nobody is likely to wish to buy. Given, however, the focus in this chapter on learning cultures and learning communities, a rather clearer route map is required and soon. Recalling the intrinsic untidiness, the messiness, of the learning community might help us to understand why.

Learning communities are untidy or messy because of their intrinsic dynamic and multifaceted nature. Learning communities are innovatively responsive to the needs of an ever changing learner cohort, especially where the learners are based in the diverse, mobile, transient, turbulent populations of the inner city. Learning communities are multi-agency and trans-disciplinary. Learning communities are responsive to new innovations in pedagogy, learning theory and information and communication technology. And, probably most important, learning communities blur the distinction between teacher and learner, between community educator and teacher, between professional practitioner and lay facilitator, between careers officer and guidance mentor and between informal and formal education. Tidy up the learning community and the risk is that it is killed off by curriculums, timetables, qualifications, accreditations, funding mechanisms, provider regulations or whatever.

Herein lies the challenge for the local management agency, be it a local school or college, a council library service, an LEA or the sub regional Learning and Skills Council: to support the development of this thriving, untidy, innovative, dynamic learning community while bringing some coherence to it. The learner needs to be able to select from a range of contexts (local school, college, learning shop, health centre, social services unit, training organisation) and, in a genuine learning community, they need to be able to mould, contribute to and receive the learning on offer. By comparison, if the teacher-learner split can be reasserted for a moment, the potential learning provider needs to be able to plan delivery in the context of provision in the locality with the comprehensive nature of delivery emerging across a geographical area rather than resting in one institution.

Within such a framework of dispersed provision, both learners and providers need to remain knowledgeable about their shared learning community. They need to be able to access, in some form, a reasonable A-Z of learning opportunities, a one stop shop, a local website or, possibly, the kind of local learner panels or forums cited earlier, such as those being developed by London Boroughs such as Brent and Enfield. In Enfield, organisations central to the delivery of key aspects of the borough's lifelong learning strategy (including schools, libraries, colleges, training providers and voluntary sector groups) have formed a steering group to co-ordinate overall delivery, established groups to work on the development of provision to fill identified gaps in activity and set up bi-annual learner forums to give expression to the voice of learners and providers beyond their immediate networks. Such route maps and forums offer a clue as to the potential role for local authorities in the future evolution of the lifelong learning project.

Uniting the citizenship, standards and lifelong learning agendas in local authorities

In the language of good ideas, few concepts have been more appealing than that variously described as 'joined up writing' or 'joined up thinking'. Few have also slipped from the limelight so quickly, possibly because of the challenges that 'joined up' approaches bring to rigid organisational and academic boundaries. Tribes and their territories, especially professionally qualified tribes, do not much warm to the multi-agency, trans-disciplinary world of joined-up-land.[11] Successful lifelong learning, and the creation of the cultures and communities that this requires, demands a change of approach, a reasonable stab at joined up practice, not to tidy up the local delivery of lifelong learning, but to provide the required coherence on both the demand and supply side of the learning equation. I want to conclude by contending that local authorities are well placed to act as the promoters of such coherence for several reasons.

First and foremost, local authorities in their local government role already house, in the guise of different directorates (libraries, leisure, regeneration, social services), many of the key players in the local lifelong learning field and they necessarily maintain relationships with other strategic providers including many in the Further Education and training sectors. Here, the local authority's role as guardian of the library service is especially important. Indeed, the moves by many local authorities to unite their library and schooling provision within single directorates, inclusive of the LEA, represent a positive practical shift which can only serve to link together learning contexts such as those provided by schools, youth services and libraries in what might be termed a joined up approach for the Learning Age.

Second, as the host organisations to Local Education Authorities, they maintain a key relationship with both the youth service and with schools, not least because of the LEA's core responsibility for the setting of school achievement targets and the monitoring of progress towards these within the context of the local Education Development Plan. If a '0+' school focused approach to lifelong learning is to be adopted and if the lifelong learning, widening participation and raising achievement agendas are to be united, then LEA's must be involved in the networking, planning and advisory support necessary to the successful creation and sustaining of any learning community and any successful local interpretation of the lifelong learning project. Moreover, many LEAs retain a key role in Adult and Community Education provision, clearly a key aspect of the lifelong learning project in every locality.

Third, local authorities offer a geographical coherence and a local brand, or a set of local brands, for the local delivery of lifelong learning. Put simply, the Enfield Learning Panel is closer to the ground than any North London body would be and its very name suggests an identity with which local learners can identify. Further, the ward framework and the area by area organisation of services provide a set of more specific community identities with which learners and potential learners are entwined and on which local authorities are based. Sub-regional organisation, such as is envisaged for the 'local' branches of the Learning and Skills Council, may provide a coherent basis for funding across a wider area and may allow for a semblance of regional planning, which is to be welcomed, but delivery, especially for reluctant learners, needs to be on a local community basis.

Fourth, as democratically elected bodies, local authorities have a key responsibility for developing the communities that their members' serve. In building participation and setting out strategies for community development it is inconceivable that any local authority should be without a lifelong learning strategy that seeks to build a learning culture in and with the community that it serves. As such, just as the LEA's work links the agendas around school achievement, widening participation and lifelong learning, the local authority's activity links the broader agendas around citizenship and community achievement to the promotion of lifelong learning.

Finally, given their democratic constitution, their access to a range of representative groups and their status as major local employers, local authorities can legitimately claim the authority to initiate and facilitate the debate around the objectives that should underpin the local community's approach to lifelong learning, objectives that are critical to matching lifelong learning provision with learner need and resource availability.

Again, the task is not easy. The organisational silos of the town hall or civic centre are as strong as those inspired by the school timetable and the qualification structure and integration is intrinsically threatening to all concerned. The silos and timetables were not built for integrated, joined up, untidy initiatives like lifelong learning. The prize, though, is worth seeking. If schools ignore the opportunities to widen participation, raise standards and build citizenship that the lifelong learning project offers and if local authorities miss the chance to assert their role as those best placed to map, co-ordinate and render coherent to potential learners the wealth of provision that the lifelong learning project will bring to their locality, they will be undermining the central objective that both share: to raise and celebrate the achievement of those individuals and groups that they serve.

[1] John Crace, *Rocking the Cradle*, in *The Guardian*, July 11 2000

[2] *Building Learning Cultures and Learning Communities*, London Borough of Enfield, Enfield LEA, 1999

[3] Tom Bentley, *Learning Beyond the Classroom*, Routledge, 1998

[4] Norman Longworth and William Keith Davies, *Lifelong Learning*, Kogan Page, 1996

[5] Maggie Farrar, *UFA Support Materials Pack*, University of the First Age, 1999

[6] Peter Mortimore, *Creating Lifelong Learners: a new and inclusive vision* (opening conference address), Institute of Education, 2000

[7] Office for National Statistics, *Adult Literacy in Britain*, The Stationery Office, 1997

[8] Jim Smith and Andrea Spurling, *Lifelong Learning: Riding the Tiger*, Cassell, 1999

[9] Social Exclusion Unit, *Bridging the Gap*, The Stationery Office, 1999

[10] Frank Sturrock, Vice-Principal at Enfield College in conversation about the changing face of post-compulsory provision. See also Barry Nalebuff and Adam Brandenburger, *Co-opetition*, HarperCollins, 1996

About the contributors

John Abbott

John Abbott is President of the 21st Century Learning Initiative, based in Washington DC and the UK. A former headteacher, he is an international advisor and prolific speaker to the UN, individual countries, companies and schools on educational issues. He is the author of many books, including *The Child is Father of the Man: how humans learn and why* (January 2000) and *The Unfinished Revolution: learning, human behaviour, community and political paradox*, with Terry Ryan (NEP, 2000).

Titus Alexander

Titus Alexander is an independent educator and author working in all phases of education. In the past he has been a university research assistant, teacher, lecturer and community worker as well as Principal Lecturer for the ILEA and General Adviser (Community Education) for the London Borough of Waltham Forest. He is a founder member of the Parenting Education & Support Forum and the Self-Esteem Network. Titus's many publications include being co-author of *Riches Beyond Price: Making the Most of Family Learning* (DEMOS, 1997) and author of *Citizenship Schools: a practical guide to education for citizenship and personal development* (Campaign for Learning, 2000).

Kay Andrews

Dr Kay Andrews OBE (Baroness Andrews) set up Education Extra, the national charity which promotes out of school hours learning, in 1992. Since 1992 Education Extra has helped well over 2000 schools to develop new activities and study support programmes ranging from specialist clubs to the national summer literacy scheme and has conducted a wide range of research and development for local and national government. Kay Andrews has a background in education policy and research and has published widely in the field of science policy, social and education policy.

Christopher Ball

Sir Christopher Ball is Chancellor of the University of Derby, a Patron of the Campaign for Learning and the founding Chairman of the Talent Foundation. In addition to chairing a number of key educational bodies, he was previously Director of Learning at the RSA and Warden of Keble College, Oxford. He is a prolific public speaker and also the author of a number of influential books and reports on learning.

Michael Barber

Professor Michael Barber is Special Adviser to the Secretary of State for Education and Employment, David Blunkett, and Head of the Standards and Effectiveness Unit at the Department for Education and Employment. A former teacher, Michael's past roles have included being Education Officer for the National Union of Teachers, Chairman of the London Borough of Hackney's Education Committee, Professor of Education and Director of the Centre for Successful Schools at Keele University and Professor of Education and Dean of New Initiatives at the Institute of Education, University of London. His current responsibilities include the National Literacy and Numeracy Strategies and tackling school failure. He has been published widely and speaks regularly on radio and television about education policy. His major publications include *The National Curriculum: A Study in Policy* (KUP 1996) and *The Learning Game: Arguments for an Education Revolution* (Indigo 1997).

Tom Bentley

Tom Bentley joined Demos as a Senior Researcher in 1997 and became its Director in 1999. He has led major Demos projects on young people, social exclusion and educational underachievement and was formerly a part-time adviser to David Blunkett, the Secretary of State for Education and Employment. His work and publications on education have attracted widespread attention and his book, *Learning Beyond the Classroom: education for a changing world*, was published to great acclaim in September 1998.

Tom Bewick

Tom Bewick joined NTO National Council as Policy Director in May 1999 and now heads up its office in London. Before that he was a policy advisor for the Labour Party, advising the Party's policy commission and David Blunkett MP, Secretary of State for Education and Employment. His earlier career was as a co-founder and Director of the Centre for Social Inclusion (CSI), and as a European policy adviser at TEC National Council. He holds both Bachelors and Masters degrees in social policy from the University of Bath.

Tony Breslin

Tony Breslin has been General Adviser (14-19 Education) in the London Borough of Enfield since September 1998. Prior to this he taught in comprehensive schools in Haringey and Hertfordshire. He is a former Chairman of the Association for the Teaching of the Social Sciences, Joint Co-ordinator of Citizenship 2000, Coordinator of the Future Education Network, an experienced examiner and a member of the DfEE's Advisory Committee on Citizenship in Post Compulsory Education. He is currently undertaking doctoral research at the University of London Institute of Education. His article is written in a personal capacity.

Guy Claxton

A Chartered Psychologist and fellow of the British Psychological Society, Guy Claxton is currently Visiting Professor of Psychology and Education at the University of Bristol Graduate School of Education. An internationally renowned writer, speaker, consultant and academic specializing in human learning, change and creativity, Guy is a member of the Royal Institution Study Group on Education, Learning and the Brain. His fifteen published books include *Hare Brain, Tortoise Mind: why intelligence increases when you think less* (1997) and *Wise Up: the challenge of lifelong learning* (1999).

Anne Evans

Anne Evans is the Chief Executive for Heads, Teachers and Industry (HTI) where she negotiates leadership placements in companies for senior educationalists. Before joining HTI in 1996 she worked for Ernst and Young Business Training Consultants and as a Vice Principal in a large community college. Ann plays a central role in developing and delivering the NPQH and LPSH programmes for head teachers. She sits on the DfEE Management Development Group and the Editorial Board for Professional Development Today and has presented evidence to the select committee on developing CPD for headteachers. She speaks regularly on school leadership and is a national judge for the leadership category in the National Teaching awards.

Bob Fryer CBE

Professor Bob Fryer is Director of New College at the University of Southampton and a non-executive Director of Ufi. Bob chairs the Government's National Advisory Group for Continuing Education and Lifelong Learning (NAGCELL) and is a trustee of the Campaign for Learning and the Lifelong Learning Foundation. He was a member of the Ufi Implementation Group and sat on the Moser Group on Adult Basic Skills. Before taking on his current roles, Bob was Principal of the Northern College for residential adult education for 15 years. His academic work embraces lifelong learning, employment and trade union organisation.

Toby Greany

Toby Greany is the Campaign for Learning's Policy and Information Director. Before joining the Campaign in 1996 he taught for five years in China, Brazil and the UK and completed an M.Ed. in Adult Education and Literacy. He has authored and co-authored a number of publications, including, most recently, *Hungry to Read: new ways to promote reading* (Campaign for Learning, 2000).

Stephen Heppel

Professor Stephen Heppel is director of ULTRALAB, Anglia Polytechnic University's globally renowned learning technology research centre in Chelmsford, which has led ICT projects such as Schools OnLine and Tesco SchoolNet 2000. In addition to his teaching role, Stephen sits on a number of task forces and committees, including the DfEE Standards Task Force and the DCMS Creative Industries Task Force, and appears regularly in the press and on TV and radio discussing education, ICT and learning.

Tony Hinkley

Tony Hinkley is Deputy Headteacher at The Ellowes Hall School, Dudley and is a member of the Executive Committee of the Secondary Heads Association. The views expressed in his chapter are a product of a SHA working group and other allies.

Bill Lucas

Bill Lucas is Chief Executive of the Campaign for Learning. An ex-Deputy Headteacher in a large community school, and the founding Director of Learning through Landscapes, Bill has a track record of innovative policy development in both schools and lifelong learning. He has written more than twenty books about education including, most recently, with Toby Greany, *Learning to Learn: the agenda for schools in the 21st Century*.

Michelle Paule

Michelle Paule has taught for 14 years in a number of county and city comprehensives as well as an Italian university. She is currently an Advanced Skills Teacher and Head of English at Peers Technology College, Oxford, and is working with Oxford Brookes University/Westminster Institute in providing training for the Excellence in Cities Gifted and Talented Pupils strand.

Ken Robinson

Ken Robinson is Professor of Creativity at the University of Warwick Business School. An internationally recognised expert in the development of creativity and human resource, he led a major national inquiry for the UK Government on creativity, education and the economy in 1998, which led to the report *All Our Futures: Creativity, Culture and Education* in 1999. He is a member of the National Advisory Committee on Creative and Cultural Education and works with many organisations, private and public, in an advisory role. His publications include *Culture, Creativity and the Young, The Arts in Future Education* and numerous articles.

Terry Ryan

Terry Ryan has been a researcher for the 21st Century Learning Initiative since 1995, and its senior researcher since 1997. In 1994 he received a fellowship to work with educational reformers and students in Poland for 15 months. In addition to writing a number of articles for the Initiative he is co-author of *The Unfinished Revolution: learning, human behaviour, community and political paradox* (with John Abbott) and *The Shadows of the Past* (a book on Polish history with Wiktor Kulerski).

Phil Street

Phil Street joined CEDC (Community Education Development Centre) in 1985 and has been its Director for five years. CEDC seeks to widen participation in learning, especially among groups that have traditionally benefited least. Before joining CEDC he worked as a senior education officer in a local education authority. He has been a member of the DfEE/Social Exclusion Unit's Policy Action Team on the role of schools in the community and an adviser to the New Deal for Communities initiative. Phil writes numerous articles and speaks regularly at conferences and training events.

Martin Stephenson

Martin Stephenson established the national charity INCLUDE and is currently a member of the Youth Justice Board and a Senior Policy Adviser to the Connexions Service National Unit. An educationalist who has specialised in working with the socially excluded, Martin was a research fellow at St. Catharine's College, Cambridge, before beginning a teaching career that has also involved working in social housing, youth justice, social services and youth work. He is writing here in his own capacity.

Mike Walton

Mike Walton has been Deputy Director of Education Extra since it was first set up and he is responsible for its pilot demonstration projects, its network and publications. Before that he spent 30 years teaching in schools in London, the Home Counties and Germany and lecturing at a Teacher Training College. During his time as Headteacher of a comprehensive school in Newham, London, he led its establishment as a community school. He is co-author of *Good Policy and Practice for the After School Hours* and author of *Family Literacy and Learning*.